Quiet Hints to Growing Preachers in my Study

Spiritual Advice for Christian Ministers

By Charles Edward Jefferson

Published by Pantianos Classics

ISBN-13: 978-1-78987-578-2

First published in 1901

Contents

Dedication

To His

Younger Brethren in the Ministry

For Whom He Craves a Blessed Life and a Glorious Work,

This Little Volume is Affectionately Inscribed by the Author

I. Wherefore All This

Please let me shut the door. We are here alone, Brethren, and we want no eavesdroppers. Human ears are sensitive; and if we do not speak in quiet tones, I fear the laity may come flying as doves to our windows. It is characteristic of human nature to be interested in what is intended for somebody else. A short time ago I invited into my study a company of laymen that we might have a confidential chat concerning certain matters relating especially to the people in the pews, but before the evening was far advanced my invited guests were crowded completely into a corner by the throng of ministers who came rushing in. I had spoken only briefly when a minister began suggesting things which laymen ought to hear, and when at last my talk was finished the most robust "Amen" which reached my ears came from the approving throat of a clergyman. I fear therefore that should our present meeting be noised abroad it would be necessary to adjourn from the study to the church auditorium and possibly to the public square: for nothing so stirs the curiosity of laymen as the things which ministers discuss in secret.

I have long wished, Brethren, to talk over with you certain things which are so delicate in their nature one hesitates to mention them, but which are of so great importance to us clergymen and to the church universal, that silence concerning them cannot be commended. What I shall say is not said as criticism but rather as suggestion and admonition. Some of you have written to me, others of you have come to see me from time to time concerning perplexities in your work, and there are other things no doubt on your mind which you have not yet had opportunity to mention. In order that we might have a good confidential talk together about these things of moment to us all, I have opened wide my study door and asked you to come in. You are all, I see, younger men than I am, and therefore I can speak with greater plainness and fuller freedom. But however frank and bold my utterance, Brethren, not one syllable shall be spoken to hurt, but every syllable to help. I am not a sour-eyed censor of ministerial morality, nor do I wish to swell the chorus of that hoarse-voiced company just now shouting the ministers' dispraise. I have no sympathy with the men who persist in the affirmation that most ministers preach what they do not believe, nor do I accept the dictum laid down with gravity by sneering judges that if preachers could only preach a little all the churches would be filled. The stormy lamentations of those who would make the Seminaries hopelessly antiquated institutions and most recent graduates anointed numskulls, are in my judgment sound and fury signifying nothing. But a man with open eyes cannot fail to see that in the ecclesiastical world, as in every other, there are stumblings and failings and fallings, and if his heart be sympathetic he cannot but wish to help his brethren avoid the pitfalls into which some have fallen and safeguard them from forms of conduct which weaken and offend. Ministers as a body are I think the best men living on the earth. I could fill a dozen evenings with praises of the pulpit saints whom I have known. In purity of motive ministers as a class surpass the lawyers, in breadth of sympathy the physicians, in fidelity to principle the editors, in self-sacrifice the merchants, in moral courage the soldiers, in loftiness of ideals the teachers, in purity of life the highest classes in our best society. This is not said boastfully but gratefully as a fact not to be disputed. But ministers to be as good as other classes of men must be better than they. No other set of men make such assumptions or bind themselves to such high ideals. A lawyer when admitted to the bar does not promise to obey the ten commandments. A physician on receiving his diploma does not agree to practice the Sermon on the Mount. Being an editor involves no assumption of fidelity to gospel principles, and merchants do not enter business announcing to the world their purpose to give their life a ransom for others. If therefore both in spirit and conduct ministers as a body were not superior to every other class of men they would be a disgrace to their profession and a scandal to the world. While all men, no matter what their calling, are under the eternal law of God, and therefore morally bound to keep the ten commandments and to live in the spirit of the Sermon on the Mount, yet as clergymen are the only men who voluntarily confess these obligations and give their life to the work of making them real to other men, it follows that more may rightfully be expected of them than from any other tribe of workers in our modern Israel.

Much is rightfully expected and much also is received. To be sure there is a scapegrace here and there, and of not a few clerical workmen there is abundant reason to be ashamed, but in a world like this, universal piety and wisdom among the professed servants of religion is as impossible to-day as it was when Jesus chose his dozen men one of whom was Judas. Taking the clerical body as a whole it is made up of honest, capable, faithful men.

But a man may be all this and still fail. There are infirmities of temper and infelicities of conduct which, while hardly falling into the category of sins, are none the less so disastrous in their effects on spiritual life as to be worthy of a place among those evils from which one should pray to be delivered. Ministers with rare exceptions are neither rogues nor hypocrites, but being human they are capable of all sorts of distorted action, and the very nature of their work exposes them to a multitude of dangers from which other men are on the whole exempt. Many a man in the ministry fails, not because he is bad, but because he has a genius for blundering. Men with ability sufficient to carry them to distinction fail to rise because of foibles and oddities which they seem unable to shake off. "O if he would only quit that!" How frequently that doleful exclamation has fallen from the lips of the despairing saints. Even slight defects in clergymen are momentous because they live always in a light as searching and intense as that which beats upon a throne. What other man in the community makes such constant self-disclosures as the minister? His eyes, lips, teeth, facial expression, voice, mind, heart, moods, all these are subjected to public scrutiny. Whatever is crooked or unchristian in him is certain to come out. The Scripture says the saints shall judge the world. It is their special province and delight to judge those who minister to them in spiritual things. Since this is so, there is reason, Brethren, why we, of all men, should walk circumspectly, redeeming the time.

II. A Mirror for Ministers

Probably no other man in the town is subjected to such a constant stream of criticism as the minister, and possibly no other man profits so little by criticism as he. This is not because of the rhinoceros quality of the ministerial skin, but because the criticism does not reach him. Those who make the fiercest onslaughts on him get in their best work when he is not in sight. Even the glib-tongued experts become silent on his approach. Other men are censured to their face. The tough meat sold by the butcher brings an immediate and audible response. The merchant who sells unsatisfactory goods must take the condemnation which is sure to come. If the editor offends in word or deed, the next mail brings him condemning letters. The mechanic who scamps his work is promptly overhauled. The servant who shirks his duties is reprimanded or dismissed. But who is bold enough to face a clergyman, and tell him of his sins?

"There's such divinity doth hedge a king,
That treason can but peep to what it would."

And there is such divinity doth hedge a preacher that dissatisfaction dares but whisper what it feels. Outside the hedge disapprobation makes wry faces and detraction does its deadly work while within the hedge the minister lives on in ignorance of his critics' strictures, untouched by what the parish thinks and says. Disgruntled men sputter at the Sunday dinner-table in the presence of their children, and women in divers places drop acidulated observations, but, alas, the man who ought to be helped by this discriminating wisdom is left to flounder in the morass into which he has fallen, and dies at last in his sins.

If, perchance, someone ventures to call the minister's attention to any one of his shortcomings, it is seldom done in such a way as to bring the needed help. A caustic cavil or poisoned fling is tucked into an envelope and sent to him unsigned, and the good man who has been told to pay no attention to anonymous letters, tosses it promptly into the wastebasket unread. An anonymous letter has little healing in its wings.

But there are occasional mortals bold enough to meet the preacher face to face. There are in almost every congregation two or three keen-eyed individuals who are determined at all hazards to be "faithful." But these persons are generally as disagreeable as they are faithful, and in their work of pulling motes their awkwardness is so exasperating as to lead the unhappy minister to consider them not ministering angels but new incarnations of that spirit of evil against which the Christian warrior must learn to stand. The ordinary self-appointed critic of ministerial character and conduct undoubtedly has a place in God's plan of creation, but what it is has not yet been definitely ascertained.

But if the anonymous bloodhounds and the professional fault-finders are useless in the work of redemption, how is a minister to be saved? Shall some sweet, sane saint call the Pastor aside and tell him gently of his sins? Possibly yes, but it is a hazardous undertaking, as many a saint has long ago discovered. A minister, like other mortals, is human and whenever pricked he bleeds. Even the best men when censured writhe and tingle and sometimes smart for many days. The smarting may generate even in a pious heart a feeling of resentment or at least of suspiciousness, so that forever afterward the relations between the Pastor and his critic are not what they were. Any minister who has ever talked plainly to a parishioner concerning his shortcomings knows that always afterward that talk has loomed up between them like a Chinese wall, giving each of them a sense of separation which could not be obliterated. The relations between a Pastor and his people are so delicate that like the finest porcelain they cannot be broken and ever be the same again. They may be mended but there is always a consciousness of the existence of the crack. Laymen who have ventured to give their Pastor from time to time quiet hints know how delicate and critical such business is. As a rule they do not pursue it far, finding relief henceforth in an interior protest against that which they do not like, and endeavoring to remember the apostolic injunction, "we then that are strong ought to bear the infirmities of the weak, and not to please ourselves."

If the improprieties and delinquencies are too numerous and flagrant to render protracted endurance a virtue the church committee sometimes acts as a tribunal before which the offending Pastor is summoned, but this usually marks the beginning of the end. It brands the minister in the eyes of the congregation as a culprit, and when once a minister's reputation for good sense or fine taste is tarnished he has already entered upon that downward road which leads to the dissolution of the pastoral relation. It is for this reason that church committees are loath to censure their minister unless driven to it by repeated indiscretions and blunderings which cry aloud for redress.

What then is a church to do? Brethren, it is a serious question. Many of us clergymen do not realize how serious it is. A congregation is at the mercy of a man, who although a minister, may have poor judgment, bad taste, a coarse nature, a blunted conscience, and a fatal gift for saying and doing the wrong thing. He may have pulpit manners which are abominable and mannerisms which are constant subtractions from his power. He may have constitutional ailments and temperamental deformities which might be reduced or cured by a course of patient treatment, but of whose existence he himself is apparently unconscious. He may be guilty of conduct which though not positively sinful is unbecoming in a man of God. Because of spiritual obtuseness he may persist in courses of action which are so flagrantly unchristian as to cause the unbelieving to blaspheme. He may become the slave of any one of a thousand hateful habits, and so difficult is it to rescue him from these tyrants, one sometimes wishes that all the ministers of Christendom could be gathered at stated intervals into spiritual hospitals especially provided for the purpose in order that every man might be critically dissected by men not afraid to lay their finger upon every blemish and excrescence, and able to burn afresh upon every heart the loftiest ideals of ministerial character and service. "A Mirror for Magistrates" is the suggestive title of a book long famous in English literature: why should there not be "A Mirror for Ministers"?

III. The Man of Macedonia

A student on emerging from the Seminary sometimes experiences a chilling surprise. The world does not seem glad that another laborer is now ready to enter the vineyard. It bustles unconcernedly along its hurried way without the slightest manifestation of interest in the youth who longs to do it service. It cares apparently nothing for his Hebrew or his Greek or even for his stores of information concerning the latest speculations of the greatest German scholars. And even for his earnest spirit which yearns to render Christ-like ministry it shows an indifference at once inexplicable and crushing. What makes this indifference well nigh intolerable is that it is the indifference of the Christian world. The Pagan world cannot be expected to take an interest in a herald of the Nazarene, but surely the Christian world will reach forth a loving hand and lift him into a place of usefulness and power. Not so. The churches are engrossed each in its own affairs, and have no time to create a sphere in which this Christian orator can exercise his gifts. Most of the churches are already supplied with leaders, and those whose pulpit is without an occupant are either feeble and fainting enterprises struggling for existence in forlorn and obscure places, or they are churches of historic dignity to whose leadership a man fresh from school cannot aspire. What shall the young man do? He cannot dig and to beg he is ashamed. There does not seem to be anything to do but to begin and live the gospel. To do this is always well, and a man ought to begin to do it before he is intrusted with a church. The division of labor has been carried far and will no doubt be carried farther, but it will never be so extended as to enable one set of Christians to preach the gospel while the other set is left to practice it. If a man expects to move men by his preaching h6 must first do a deal of living, and the sooner he begins to live the better. Where can a man find larger opportunity for the exercise of that faith and hope and love, of that patience, persistency and courage of which he intends through all the years to speak than just in that dark and troubled period which for many men immediately follows the completion of the Seminary course? If a man is to hold up Abraham as an example worthy of imitation why should he shrink from going out not knowing whither he goes? And if he proposes to spend his life in teaching men to believe that the just must walk by faith, why should he not do a little of that sort of walking himself? If he believes in the principle announced by Jesus that every one who asks receives why does he not proceed to put that principle to the test.

A man who intends to preach the Gospel ought to learn early that God is no respecter of persons, and that a student of theology is not allowed to enter the Kingdom by a road specially constructed for his own tender feet. Anything like favoritism or coddling is abhorrent to the spirit of the Christian religion. Christ thrusts a cross into a man's face and holds it there. Accursed is every policy which attempts to hide it or take it away. Men who prepare for the ministry ought to have no advantages given them which are denied to their fellows. They should work for their education as hard as do the men who prepare for journalism or medicine or law. Every indulgence and plum intended to make the way into the ministry more attractive than that which leads into the other professions ought to be feared and discarded. If this reduces recruits for the ministry so much the better for the churches. What can organized Christianity accomplish unless its leaders are stalwart and tough? Men are not going to endure hardness as good soldiers of Christ when once installed as pastors of churches unless they have been trained to do this from their youth. No one who is not willing to work like a slave through as many years as may be necessary to fit him for his work is worthy to stand before the world as an ordained expounder of the message of the Son of God.

After a man has secured his schooling then let him make himself a place in which to work. If all the doors are shut let him open one. If he cannot do this he is not needed. No man can open men's hearts for the Gospel who is too weak to open a door for himself into the ministry. It is not a diploma which proves a man's right to be a preacher, but a spiritual temper and a moral stamina like unto those of the Apostles. Occasionally one catches a whimpering tone in the talk of young men looking for a church. In their judgment they are badly used. The churches do not appreciate the sacrifices these men have made. If some church does not speedily repent and give a call then these ill-used prophets will shake off the dust of their feet against them and will not preach at all! All such whining proceeds from a heart which is not right. The young physician in making a place for himself in a world already overcrowded expects a long-drawn struggle, and he is seldom disappointed. In many cases years of poverty and privation He between him and the shining goal on which his hungry eyes are set. The average lawyer fights a long and tremendous battle — so do the journalist and professor, the architect and artist, the merchant and musician. Every man is left to make for himself his own place in the world, and why should a minister be favored above his brethren?

While in the Seminary he heard the world calling for him, and in his dreams a noble church stood up, glorious and imploring, and would not let him rest. But now when he is ready the church has melted into air, and in his disappointment he is ready to believe that all things are as vain and empty as the baseless fabric of a dream. Let him remember that his vision was similar to that of the Apostle Paul. The man of Macedonia who would not let Paul sleep for his constant cry, "Come over and help us," was nowhere to be seen when Paul reached the shores of Europe. Paul could not find him at Neapolis nor even at Philippi. Outside the Philippian gate a few women listened to the first Christian sermon preached in Europe, but the "man of Macedonia" was conspicuous for his absence. Europe was preoccupied with her business and pleasures, and it was only by the boldest and most persevering exertions that the apostle succeeded in opening a door in any European city. Europe needed the Gospel — she did not want it. The world to-day needs young men equipped to preach the Gospel, but it does not want them. Like Saul of Tarsus they must fight their way into public recognition assisted by some good Barnabas or Silas who is always present to lend a helping hand, and instead of railing at a world which is slow to crown them they must build for themselves the thrones from which they are to judge the tribes of Israel.

IV. Which Door?

It is well for a man not to be too heavily weighted with theories at the beginning of his career. Otherwise he may become so entangled as to be crippled for life. Man proposes but God disposes, and the manner of his disposition is often marvelous in our eyes. Precious time may be squandered in a fruitless endeavor to bring the Almighty into conformity to human expectations. It is natural for a minister to have his preferences, but he should not insist on these when it becomes evident that Heaven prefers something else. He should not draw a circle round a limited area of land and say, "Up to the circumference of that circle shall my activity be felt but no further." A man who says that needs to reread his New Testament. The men who crowd into favored localities already overstocked with ministers and stand all the years idle, bitterly complaining because no church has hired them, eking out a precarious livelihood by snapping up occasional opportunities to preach in pulpits temporarily vacant, are not men to be trusted with the guidance and training of Christians. Ministers of the Gospel should be made of more heroic stuff. Old men out of whom the years have taken the lunge and the fire may be forgiven for such conduct; but for a young man to hover round a particular city like a moth round a candle, forgetful that he is ordained to be a light in a place that is dark, is an exhibition of selfishness which ought to doom him in the estimation of the Christian public. A man ought to preach not where he wants to preach but where he can preach.

Nor is it wise to say, "I will begin with a small church and none other," or "I will start in the country and later on come to the city." The theory held by many that every minister should begin in a small church in the country is the creation of the closet and not to be universally accepted. Let a minister begin where he can. Some men are more mature at twenty than others at forty. Why insist on a narrow field if the Lord of the vineyard points out a wide one? And why insist on staying in the country if circumstances mould themselves into a trumpet through which a voice is heard saying, "Arise, go into the city and it shall be told thee what thou must do?" Ministers as well as laymen ought to surrender themselves to the guidance of the Spirit, and in the fire of the Spirit all opinions and theories will be as chaff. A young man ought to go through the widest door which swings on its hinges before his face. But to sit down before a narrow open door refusing to enter it because of a hope that a wider door will some day be opened is the act of a man whose life is guided not by the Holy Spirit but by his own unholy ambitions.

But suppose a field is hard, shall a young man take it? Why not? All fields when known at first hand are hard. The easy fields of which we sometimes read exist only in the imagination. Each heart knows its own bitterness and each parish has its own snags. The minister whose life seems to be one grand, sweet song is found to be a heavily-laden burden-bearer when one comes close enough to hear his heart-beats. There is not that difference in parishes which the unthinking observer imagines. Conspicuous advantages have their manifold subtractions, and striking losses have their surprising compensations. No one man can have everything, even in the ministry. If a man is deprived of privileges in the country so does a man pay dearly for living in the city. If a small church has its difficulties and distresses, a large church is not free from complications and perplexing problems. If a man is afraid of fields which are hard never let him think of becoming a minister. A field reputedly hard ought to have peculiar fascination for a man who has grit. If a dozen men have failed in it the charm ought to be all the greater. Woe to the minister who is looking for an easy job! There is more hope for a fool than for him. And as for the church being small, that is nothing against it. It is the glory of a small church that it can grow. To see a church grow is one of the deepest joys a minister can know. What greater privilege could a young man ask than that of taking a little church and by a process of nurture carried on through patient years causing that church through the blessing of God to develop until it becomes the crown of the community, the center of wide regions whose people look to it for impulse and guidance? What a glowing, gladdening task compared with that of a man who takes a large church whose limit of growth has been already reached, and for which the years contain no brighter prospect than that of successfully resisting the processes of disintegration and decay!

It is not becoming in young men fresh from school to be over particular about either geography or finance. A man cannot tell how much he is worth in the pulpit by computing the amount of money he has expended on his education. Nor ought he with a flourish dictate to churches the lowest terms at which his services can be secured. A man with a wife and ten children may be excused for making sundry inquiries concerning the salary, but a young man unencumbered should seek first of all a chance to work, and finding this, all necessary things will be added unto him. The men who put salary first and church second are usually the men whose salary never increases. A man who will not preach at all unless some church puts into his palm the precise sum which he thinks his preaching worth ought to be left to die with all his sermons in him. Young men with the ribbon on their diploma still unfaded ought not to go into the market shouting — "So many sermons for so many dollars!" The supreme question is, "Where can I work? Where will the followers of Christ give me a chance to work? Where can I make my life count for most in the extension of the kingdom?" The man who goes into the world with these queries burning in his heart will not long be without a congregation, nor will he lack shelter and raiment and food.

If however the time of waiting is longer than he anticipated let him not be despairful. If one door after another is slammed in his face, let him keep on knocking. If one field after another fades from his eyes, let him keep on seeking. If these disappointments move him he was never foreordained for the ministry. Men who are worthy of the Christian pulpit will get into it though they climb to it over obstacles high as the Alps, and over Himalayas of disappointment. It may be necessary for a time to earn one's bread by secular employment; but if the man has been chosen by the Lord, he will sometime, somehow, somewhere overcome the last opposing circumstance and enter into the joy of ministerial service. A Scotchman who knocked in vain while a young man at the door of twenty-three churches and filled ten years with patient waiting, became at last one of the most distinguished and influential preachers of his generation.

V. Starts Good and Bad

"All's well that ends well," but in order that one may end well there should be a good beginning. A bad start in a pastorate is disastrous. The blunders of the first few weeks may throw a shadow over many years. When the minister goes into his new parish he ought to give himself at once to his supreme task, feeding the sheep. Whatever else a minister may be, he is first of all a shepherd. To feed the people entrusted to his keeping is his first and most urgent duty. If he attends first of all to this and keeps on attending to it blessed is he.

But if he begins, as many a man has begun, by endeavoring to show the sheep what a wonderful man he is, he will wreck the peace of many days. If, for instance, he spends his first Sunday in the discussion of some such useless theme as, "The relation of the Pastor to the Church," the hungry sheep in spite of all their looking up will go away unfed. Not even a goat can find nutriment in any such juiceless discussion. A minister is a servant and it ill becomes a servant to come into the presence of those he serves with an analysis of abstract relationships on his lips. When we hire a servant to feed us we want him to put the dishes on the table: what he thinks of our relations to him and of him to us will come out in the way in which he does his work. If he postpones the dinner in order to enlighten us concerning our mutual obligations we are in no mood to appreciate his ideas or to accept his conclusions. A servant who calls attention to himself rather than to the dinner is a servant who does not understand his business. The minister who on the first Sunday magnifies himself by telling his hearers what he has a right to expect of them and what they may properly demand of him, is guilty of an indiscretion for which he may be forgiven, but which a man of tact will not commit. Do what he may, the minister on his opening Sundays is sufficiently in the public eye, and it is the part of wisdom for him to obliterate himself so far as possible in the humble work of feeding the sheep. To keep the eyes of a congregation steadfastly fixed on Christ is wisdom always, but it is never quite so important as on those first searching Sundays when eyes as yet untrained to love are prone to find and magnify defects. "A mother does not read to her newborn baby an essay on the obligations of maternity—she feeds it:" so spoke one of the greatest of modern preachers to a company of students years ago, his contention being that a preacher who goes before a new congregation with a discussion of mutual obligations is as foolish as a woman would be who should postpone the feeding of her baby for a dissertation on the relations of parent and child.

Nor should the new minister convert his earliest sermons into programs of parochial work. We are living in a driving age, but it is possible for a clergyman to drive too fast. A minister of the Gospel is not a sheep-driver, but a sheep-feeder. The former inevitably gets himself into trouble, especially if he manifests his driving propensities the first week. For a stranger to come into a parish and proceed forthwith to tell his hearers what he expects them to do borders closely on the impertinent. Why not first of all feed the sheep? To feed sheep does not smack of presumption nor does it stir up opposition. Sheep like to be fed. They never resist. When repeatedly fed by the same shepherd they will follow him whithersoever he leads them. He can shear them again and again, and weave their wool into all sorts of lovely patterns for the glory of God, but when the new minister attempts to shear a flock of strange sheep the first day before noon he usually precipitates a furious scrimmage which is likely to leave the shepherd discomfited and out of breath. Many a man has complained bitterly of the foolishness and stubbornness of his sheep, who would have had no trouble had he only placed the feeding before the shearing. No sentence more momentous for clergymen lies between the lids of the Bible than the little sentence which too many of the successors of the Apostles have in every age overlooked. "Feed my sheep."

Nor should there be undue haste in knocking to pieces the contrivances which the former minister created. These things should be allowed to stand, if not forever, at least till day after to-morrow. Other men have labored and the new minister should enter into their labors, not stamp upon them. To begin afresh as though all who have gone before him were drones or dunces is not commendable. Every minister must do his work in his own way, and it is natural that a man should feel himself capable of making sundry improvements over the methods of his predecessor, but this predecessor was probably not so great a blunderbuss as he appears to the man who comes after him. No matter with what wisdom and fidelity a man may labor he leaves a parish in an unsatisfactory condition. Everything is incomplete, much is perverted and wrong, there is more or less friction, appalling inefficiency, and on all sides a wide chasm yawns between the actual and ideal. A new man on coming into such a field — especially if he be without experience — is apt to feel that things would not be as they are had his predecessor done his work with greater ability and wisdom. Upon this departed man as upon a scapegoat are saddled all the sins of the parish, and the new Pastor, eager to prove himself superior to all who have gone before him, proceeds to break to pieces the parochial machinery, and to create a new set of agencies which will usher in the golden age. Poor man, later on he will discover under a juniper tree that he is no better than his fathers.

Do not be in a hurry, brethren, to revolutionize the constitution and bylaws of your parish before your parish learns to trust your judgment and comes to occupy your view-point. You may be able to introduce an improvement here and there as the years come and go, but please wait until after dinner before you start. There is a conservative instinct implanted by the Almighty in the human heart for the purpose of safe-guarding the world from the folly of fussy reformers, and against this instinct as against a Damascus blade a minister hurls himself if feverishly ambitious to make all things new. Instead of splitting former societies and methods into kindling wood why not be content to feed the sheep? Feeding sheep involves no perils, whereas kindling-wood may lead to a conflagration.

VI. The Foremost of the Demons

To all the sons of Adam there comes the temptation to be lazy, and therefore let the minister beware. It is not true, as some men think, that all clergymen are lazy, but it is true that they like other men are tempted, and alas, too many of them succumb. Intellectual indolence is far more common than is generally supposed. Mental activity, except in rare cases, is not congenital, but an achievement. The average man is prone to follow the line of least resistance, and unless the angels of his better nature repeatedly bring him back, he will wander far away from close and continuous mental toil.

Many a minister is indolent without realizing how indolent he is. It is possible to entertain demons as well as angels unawares. Not infrequently a man will fuss and bustle over miscellaneous matters, giving the parish the impression of tremendous diligence, while all the time his intellect is a dawdler at its work. A man intellectually lazy will do anything rather than whip his mind to mental exercise. He will scamper over the parish and astonish the county by the number of his parochial visits. He will multiply organizations and manipulate them with a dexterity quite amazing. He will engage in all sorts of schemes and enterprizes to maintain the interest of the people, rather than buckle down to hard, exacting, redeeming mental labor. There are many Bible sentences appropriate for mottoes to be hung on the wall of the minister's study, but not one them has in it a greater wealth of needed warning than the Hebrew proverb —

"Go to the ant, thou sluggard,
Consider her ways and be wise."

It was the conviction of the Hebrew sages that idleness is ruinous, and that if a man prefers ease to labor his poverty will come as a robber and his want as an armed man. The robber has already overtaken many a clergyman and the armed man is on the track of many another.

What other man has such urgent reasons for being diligent as a minister? If he is indolent his sin will find him out, and so will everybody else. Other men can more easily conceal their mental sloth for most of them do their work as it were in a comer. But the minister is a public character and when he speaks whatever rust is on his mind is seen. A scraggy, scrambling prayer, a raveled, faded style, a juiceless, pithless sermon, what are these but weeds in the garden of a man who has folded his mental hands? No man can long be interesting in the pulpit who does not think. No man can think wisely who does not study. Constant mental application is the price a minister must pay for power. When men cross the deadline under seventy it is ordinarily because they have ceased to develop new cells in the gray matter of their brain. They may have been students once but their early studies cannot save them. A parish soon discovers when the minister is trusting to his diploma and has put his mind to bed.

The necessity for unceasing labor lies in the nature of the minister's work. He is a public teacher always teaching. If he spoke less frequently his words would carry greater weight. He does not get credit for the ability and worth which he actually possesses, for nothing so dulls the sense of appreciation as familiarity. Any man of intelligence endowed with a gift of expression can preach one sermon. Many men can preach seven. A few men can preach seven times seven. But seventy times seven is the work of every preacher. It is this incessant creation of new sermons which constitutes the crowning test. How to keep the reservoir full — that is the tormenting problem. Nothing short of Herculean labor will solve it. Much of the charm of public speech lies in the freshness of the speaker's accents, in the novelty of his cadences, in the newness of his view-point, in the surprises of his rhetoric, in the unexpected disclosures of his personality as revealed in his mannerisms. But to a minister all these charms are denied. His voice, rhetoric, conceptions, figures, oddities, soon become a tale that is told, and he has nothing to rely on but the earnestness of his spirit and the energy of his thought. Laymen forget this when they compare clergymen with interesting speakers whom they hear but once. They hear a man speak at a banquet or on the rostrum, and go home saying, "Ah, if we could have preaching like that! What a brainy and interesting man!" In all probability he is no brainier or brighter than their preacher. Let this fascinating speaker speak ten times to the same audience and his brilliancy will fade a little. Let him give fifty addresses and his freshness will vanish as the dew. Let him speak five hundred times and he might turn out to be as dull and stupid as a preacher. A man may be brilliant once or twice, but not all the time. Nothing grows stale so soon as brilliancy. Learning may overwhelm at first but after we have lived with it for a season we cease to be impressed. Eccentricities of voice and gesture are delicious on their first appearance, but by and by they become intolerable. If the editors and professors and college presidents and other critics who say and write bold things against the pulpit should attempt to discourse twice a week to the same congregation for ten or twenty years they might find themselves as prosy and stale and repetitious as the luckless culprits they now condemn. If then the industrious can hardly stand what shall the lazy do?

Get out of the pulpit or go to work. To be a preacher and a preacher whom the years cannot wear thin, a man must be a painstaking, indefatigable, everlasting worker. He must have a genius for toil. He must be willing to drudge and dig and grind. He must lay out his lines of study and pursue them doggedly and unconquerably through the years. He must forsake cheap papers and beware of books published for mental babes. He must trounce his mind whenever he catches it dawdling or slouching or lounging. He must quit pottering over incidentals and conundrums and wrestle with the great doctrines and dragons. He must give himself soul and body to his work with the devotion and fidelity of a slave whose heart has been redeemed by a master who renders to every man according to his work, and creates a heaven for every soul to whom he says, "Well done!"

VII. Cowardice

If a minister is willing to live laborious days he is in the way of being saved but his salvation is not assured. He may be stricken down in the midst of arduous labor by cowardice. It is easy to call preachers cowards.

Cowardice is the sin of which they have been accused from the beginning. It is an ugly insulting word, and to hurl it has been the pastime of all enemies of the church.

But it is easier to call a man a coward than to prove him one. To some men a man is always a dastard who refuses to do what they think he ought to do. That makes swift work of a man who must be gotten rid of. If you cannot answer his argument or understand his conduct call him a coward and leave him.

Now it is impossible for a minister to do everything which every man would like to see him do, or to say everything which men who are self-constituted judges insist that he must say. He must be guided by the Holy Spirit so far as he can ascertain what this guidance is, but even when following the manifest leading of the Spirit he is sure to disappoint and nettle persons who follow nothing but their passions, prejudices and whims. To many men in Palestine Jesus was the greatest coward in Hebrew history. And really they could make out a strong case against him. He declined to answer plain questions which the crowd put to him. He avoided taking sides in contentions of national importance. He refused to strike a blow at the Roman Empire, the embodiment of all villainy and the oppressor of God's people. Repeatedly he dodged his enemies in order to save his life, and he maintained a silence oftentimes which it was impossible to justify or explain. So it seemed to men who stood close to him and studied his career. But now that we behold his life in its true perspective we see how egregiously mistaken his maligners were, for in him we behold courage at its climax, the very incarnation of moral heroism. No true man can live a faithful life without appearing to men of less insight and wisdom a recreant and coward.

But nevertheless the temptation to ministerial cowardice is genuine and constant. A man may be a coward without knowing it. The greatest cowards are often the most confident of their heroism. It is true, as Thomas Fuller used to say, that there is much terra incognita in a man's own heart. This is true even of men given to introspection and patient self-examination. Satan gives one convincing reason why his chosen course is best, and takes him along the downward course so gradually he is not conscious of the descent.

Surely no minister can be other than a coward unless strength be given him from above. All things conspire to make him calculating and faint-hearted. Civilization is built on the principle that the chief end of man is to please. All society recognizes this. Well-bred people are trained not to say anything in the parlor that contradicts or hurts. The commercial world is built on the same foundation. The merchant lives to please his customers. He caters to their wishes, he anticipates their wants. He bends to every whim and mood, puts up with their criticisms and unreasonablenesses, makes himself a swift-footed servant, and counts himself successful if, at any sacrifice of personal wish or comfort, he can sell his goods. Hotel managers live to please their guests. What any guest desires that is the thing which he shall have, for hotel guests must be humored. After people have been petted, indulged and flattered by those who serve them through the week they are in no mood to be crossed or rebuked by a man in the pulpit on Sunday. They do not want to be reminded of their sins, nor do they relish the personal, passionate appeal for self-crucifixion; and the preacher knowing this is in constant peril of tempering his message to their wishes. If the failure to speak with sufficient plainness of sin — a failure widespread and notorious — is not due to cowardice, how shall we explain it?

A preacher is a leader of thought. More light is continually breaking out of the Bible. The facts of our religion never change, but the interpretation of these facts widens with the process of the suns. Sacred phraseology grows antiquated and must be discarded, ancient conceptions must be left behind. But many Christians do not read. Still fewer of them think. In every congregation there are good men and women who cling to the old phrases and the old interpretations long after they have become obsolete to the world of thinking men. They are suspicious of new terms and alarmed by new expositions and fear exceedingly lest the ark of the Lord be upset. What is the preacher to do? To hurt an ignorant saint is not pleasant and to mar the peace of a congregation is distressing, and yet the minister as leader of God's people must often do what the Man of Galilee did, shock the sensibilities of the pious by tearing old traditions to tatters. A leader of thought must follow the unmistakable guidance of the Spirit no matter what commotion may be stirred up in his parochial teapot.

It is hazardous to lay one's finger on any man and say, "Thou art a coward!" But when one sees how many giant evils are intrenched in our Christian civilization, and how many injustices on every side go unrebuked and unredressed, he cannot suppress misgivings which keep rising in his heart that the clergy as a whole have failed to exhibit the dauntless daring of the Man who once drove a pack of mercenary pedlers from the court of the Jerusalem temple. No more magnificent company of heroes have added luster to the ages than the intrepid warriors who have led the world from Christian pulpits, but when we read the history of the last nineteen hundred years and see how closely we have reproduced the bloody record of the Hebrew people, the sons in each generation building the sepulchers of the prophets whom the fathers killed, the conviction is borne in upon us that fewer of these tragedies would have come to pass if more religious leaders had bravely followed in their day and generation the light which the Holy Spirit was willing to bestow. One likes to believe that if every minister of the Gospel would speak out clearly the word of the Lord as it is made known to him, the church would have a continuous and joyous progress into Christian truth, and Christian history would not be what it has thus far been, a series of vast upheavals and reigns of terror, every dawn being wild with thunder-peals and every forward step marked by a new Golgotha.

Brethren, have you been silent concerning the colossal evils, the burning questions of our day? Silence is often the coward's cave. Have you struck evil with all your might, not the evil of patriarchal times but the evil which has lifted itself in your own parish? Have you gone on boldly in front of your people, imposing broad views on narrow hearts, endeavoring to lead both young and old into the new conceptions and interpretations which modern scholarship has forced upon the world? If you have not done these things it might be well to ask yourselves the reason Why.

VIII. Impatience

But it is possible to be too bold. All virtues when pushed too far degenerate into vices. Excessive boldness is recklessness, and recklessness wrecks a church. Some ministers are so afraid of being cowards they make themselves a nuisance by marching always on the war-path. They count a Sunday lost on which they do not preach a new crusade. Denunciation is their forte, and to scalp a hoary-headed sin is the aim of every sermon. But the human heart cannot live on anathemas. In the economy of preaching as in that of Nature thunderbolts have their place, but in the pulpit as in Nature there must be abundant sun and seasons filled with bloom and holy calm. The twenty, sixth chapter of Matthew's Gospel must be followed by the fourteenth chapter of John. A man may be courageous when not trampling abominations under his feet. One may mistake an undue development of the red Indian in him for a manifestation of saving grace. Spunk is good, but the servant of the Lord must be something more than fighting-cock or bull-dog. Evils cannot be battered into dust by the ceaseless lashings of vociferous tongues: they are disintegrated by the atmosphere created by the unfolding of great ideas. Ministers must be patient.

When William Pitt declared that the quality most essential for a successful Prime Minister is Patience, he gave utterance to words which contain a hint for every man whose business it is to work with men. No man either in church or state can carry beneficent enterprises to their consummation who lacks a patient spirit. Probably no other single sin works such havoc in the Christian church as the impatience of her ministers.

It is characteristic of average human nature to move but slowly toward those goals upon which Christ bids men set their eyes. It is likewise human to cling to customs old and tried, rather than to enter upon paths which are new. It is a minister's work to lead, not simply one man, but a company of men from one position to another, and then another, along that upward and difficult road, and unless his spirit is held in firm restraint he will not be able to brook delays or endure the oppositions and retrogressions which are sure to come.

A leader of men must be patient with them. Even the malcontents and the cranks must not be snubbed or squelched. Some ministers cannot endure the presence of even one man whose heart is not with them, and proceed forthwith to harry him out of the parish. Unless this man is gotten rid of there can be no peace in the ministerial bosom. But in rooting out the offender what damage may be wrought. The tares always grow close to the wheat, and one cannot be uprooted without damaging the other. If a preacher is only patient, Death may come to his assistance, and remove the tare without touching the wheat. A beautiful, indispensable friend is Death! He saves preachers from despair when they see certain parishioners flourish like a green bay tree. If men's sins are to be patiently endured, much more worthy of gentle consideration are their stupidities and frailties. It is the province of the preacher to see the New Jerusalem hovering in the air, but he ought not to break the skulls of the saints in his haste to get the fair city squarely located on the earth. Every man who sees visions and dreams dreams cannot but yearn to have his parish far different from what it is, and to change whatever seems to hinder the free development of church life along the lines of largest usefulness is certainly a laudable ambition. But in making changes a minister should ponder Josh Billings's counsel to young men, "If you want to get along quick, go slow." Because a thing is good it does not follow the parish must have it before sunset. That the preacher wants it is not sufficient reason why the parish should bow sweetly and instantly to his will. Things which are accepted willingly are the only things which a minister can establish in his parish to the edification of his people. Whatever is forced upon them, even though excellent in itself, causes an irritation which offsets whatever service it might have been expected to render. The momentary gratification which comes to a man who succeeds in having his way is poor compensation when it is secured at the sacrifice of the sympathy and good will of the people. A minister ought to learn how to stand and wait. If a man is convinced in his own mind that a certain step is advantageous for his people, and his people will not let him take it, let him not lie down and turn his face to the wall, watering his couch with his tears, neither let him stride stormfully across his people's wishes doing the thing of which they disapprove, but let him be resolute and patient.

"Men's souls are narrow; let them grow,
My brothers, we must wait."

A congregation is composed of pupils in various stages of development, and the wise preacher remembers this in the preparation of his sermons. The congregation is a flock of sheep. Many sheep can walk but slowly, some of the lambs must be carried, while an occasional old ram must be dealt with with discretion. It is the business of the shepherd to be ahead of his sheep, but he must not be so far in advance as to be out of sight. If he gets too far ahead a sense of superiority may take possession of him, and this may pass into a feeling of contempt. New found truth — says Carlyle — like new got gold burns the pockets until it is spent. The clerical miner who has been digging gold all week coins it and throws it down before his people on Sunday with an air which says: "If you do not accept this you are benighted!" Ministers should imitate the Holy Spirit and guide men into the truth. Too many of them try to take their hearers into truth on the jump. If a man has advanced ideas, he must give his people time to catch up with them. Many a good man in his eagerness to display his emancipation from the past has by his headlong impetuosity closed the hearts of his best people, and rendered impossible the achievement of that which was dearest to his heart.

Brethren, study the life of Jesus for the high art of reticence and reserve. "I have many things to say unto you but you cannot bear them now:" so he said and says. The mind cannot be forced. New truth cannot be hammered into the heart even by a man fresh from the Seminary. Old interpretations are sloughed off and new conceptions find entrance into the mind only as the affections are enriched and the life is enlarged. This work is done by the Holy Spirit and like all the work of God it is carried on by processes which require time for their completion. If a man is willing to speak out in love the truth which has become certain to his soul, and has sense enough to abstain from scornful words of by-gone teachers and traditional teachings, he can ordinarily preach what his people need without the slightest danger of precipitating an ecclesiastical earthquake.

Patience then is the queen of the ministerial virtues. Like the farmer the preacher is engaged in a work which demands the exercise of all the powers of long-suffering diligence and protracted wakefulness and waiting. It is noteworthy that our Lord saw in the slow and stately operations of Nature a revelation of the processes of spiritual growth, and to Nature we must go for rare disclosures of the secrets of successful spiritual labor. To his disciples then and now and always the Son of God makes this declaration,

"In your patience ye shall win your souls."

IX. Clerical Hamlets

A wide reader of ministerial biography has declared that "a gently complaining and fatigued spirit is that in which evangelical divines are very apt to pass their days." If this be true we have found an explanation of many a pulpit failure. For no man can be masterful as teacher or leader whose spirit is either plaintful or fatigued. The message of the preacher is glad tidings of great joy, and unless there is joy in the herald his message will have a broken wing. Whatever else a minister may be he must be pre-eminently a man of good cheer. His presence must be a constant exhortation, Rejoice, again I say unto you Rejoice!

But who has not known ministers whose voice and face seemed to be always saying, Let us cry! Such a man goes about shutting up all the Eastern windows which look toward the sun. In his presence the singing swallows become silent and the brooks of morning dry up. Those who sit in darkness and in the shadow of death find no deliverance in him for he is in darkness himself. He abides not in the light because there is no light in him.

It is surprising how many ministers live in a petulant and peevish mood. Even men who are able to carry a serene exterior are often found on closer contact to be morbid and glum. Life is going hard with them. Things are all wrong. They are not appreciated. Parish interests are in a snarl. The world has not treated them fairly. And so in private they bleed and pout and whine.

The age gives such men no end of trouble. It is a materialistic, sordid age and they wear themselves out shrieking, "The time is out of joint!" The world has grown indifferent to spiritual voices, and as it rushes to destruction the poor preacher looks helplessly on and blubbers. But why these tears? Ours is not the only materialistic age. When was there an age since the great flood that was not more materialistic than this one? The apostles grappled with a generation more sodden far and brutish than the one now on the stage, and not a whimper escaped from one of them. Preachers are not ordained to preach to golden ages but to ages of stone and bronze and iron. A minister sometimes gets the impression that his town is wicked above all others. Its inertia and stupidity first sadden him and then make him mad. He rails at it. He cuffs it as though it were a wayward child. In a town of greater intelligence his work, he thinks, would receive a more generous recognition!

But is not such complaining unmanly? All places are wicked. Men who live in great cities are ready to confess that the devil has made the city his headquarters; but men who live in little country towns declare that towns are even worse than the cities. Sodom and Gomorrah lurk under the thin crust of civilization everywhere. A man engaged in religious work soon discovers that the world is possessed of seven devils. But this discovery should not dash or damp him. If humanity wbre clothed and in its right mind the occupation of the preacher would be gone. It is because men have lost their way that a guide is needed. It is because men are sick unto death that God has raised up physicians. They that are whole have no need of a physician. The more godless a community the greater need of a man of God to work in it. Saul of Tarsus was not daunted by the rottenness of the cities of Asia. Their squalor and wretchedness made him all the more desirous of preaching the gospel in the world's darkest center, the godless metropolis of the Roman empire. Paul saying, "I must also see Rome:" our faint-hearted modern brother wailing, "This place is wicked, I must get out of it" — O what a fall is there, my countrymen!

Sometimes it is not the world in general but a man's own parish which causes him to wince and quail. A newspaper gets on his track and misreports him. His sermons are garbled and his actions are misjudged, and the mangled son of thunder goes about bleeding at every pore. A man too thin-skinned to stand newspaper criticism is not a fit man to lead the Lord's army. A newspaper is frequently the most unprincipled and merciless of antagonists, and when controlled by men who are hostile to the church it may make the clergyman the target for continuous abuse; but a minister who is wise will never enter into a controversy with a newspaper. To be beaten with a few stinging sentences is not so painful as to be beaten with a Roman scourge, and it was after being whipped with a Roman scourge that Paul and Silas sang. If a minister cannot sing after being trounced by the most merciless reporter who ever poured bad blood into ink, he should get out of the pulpit and seek a position where thin skin is not a hindrance to duty.

Or the anonymous coward instead of attacking him in a newspaper may stab him through the mail. Two or three anonymous letters will cause some men to swell up as though they had been bitten by tarantulas. For days afterward they smart and moan, and try they never so hard to hold it back, more or less of their hurt feeling trickles into their next Sunday's discourses.

The criticism may not be written but spoken. It may float through the atmosphere in the shape of poisonous rumors. A set of liars by attending strictly to business can fill an entire community with aerial hints of their personality, and a minister who is disposed to take notice of every word spoken against him will be kept in a state of chronic resentment.

Men may resist him not only by their words but by their actions. This opposition may come from members of his own church. All Christians are called to be saints, but in many of them the saintship has not passed beyond the germinal stages Even church officials may surpass the heathen Chinese for ways that are dark and tricks that are vain, and the luckless preacher repeatedly outwitted and imposed upon by men whose moral development is as yet embryonic may have such a budget of wrongs to talk about that these wrongs are more frequently on his lips than the truths in which he is supposed to live. Nothing is more nauseating than a grown baby forever dwelling on his wrongs. A minister who constantly appeals for sympathy is a minister whom everybody wants to get away from. One instinctively shrinks from the man who as soon as he gets you alone proceeds to take off the poultices with which he has bandaged his soul that you may see how badly he has been hurt.

How can a man who snivels preach the gospel? Clouds and darkness are round most men and it is the preacher's business to let the sunlight in. A congregation' needs nothing so much as sun. Melancholy is a disease both contagious and deadly. One man may poison with the virus of his despondency an entire community.

Therefore, O man of God, quit your pining. Stop your moping. Put an end to your brooding. Get out of the slough of despond. Cut down your cypresses and willows. Burn up your sermons with sobs in them. "Be converted." "Be not afraid." "Be of good cheer." "Rejoice and be exceeding glad." This is the language of Christ and his apostles. Yours it is to

"Clothe the waste with dreams of gain,
And on midnight's sky of rain
Paint the golden morrow."

X. Despondency

The prime causes of despondency are three, nerve exhaustion, protracted delays, unfounded expectations. A minister is subjected to an incessant nervous strain. As executive officer he is harassed by the details and friction of church administration. As pastor he is in constant contact with the sorrowing and the sick. The poor also are always with him. He knows as few men do how the other half lives. Numberless needy men and women slip up to him in the crowd and by their touch draw virtue from him. It is often with a dizzy head and a sick heart that he goes into the pulpit Sunday morning to make a still heavier draft upon his vital forces. The world does not know how great a tax upon a sensitive man an earnest sermon is. No man can vitalize other men without devitalizing himself. Sermons that heal and lift have in them the red blood of the preacher's heart. He may save others, himself he cannot save. It is cruel, says London's greatest preacher, to ask a man to preach twice in one day. Only men to whom preaching is the shedding of blood can understand so bold a saying. It was physical exhaustion which cast Elijah under a juniper tree and drew from his heroic lips the unmanly cry "It is enough!" The tree has a crowd still under it suffering from a like exhaustion.

But a man who lives under a juniper tree cannot preach Gospel sermons. The tree will affect the quality of his voice. A juniper tree voice is an abomination to God and man. It will also control his choice of subjects. He will select themes which give large room for lamentations. Even jubilant texts he will drag through the mire of his gloom. No matter what tune he attempts he will play it with the tremolo stop. Whatever sermonic gold is cast into the fire will come out a calf and a sick calf at that. A disheartened man takes the heart out of everybody else. Unless he is resisted he will drag the whole parish under his juniper tree.

Such a man needs food for the nerves. Let him get out into God's out-of-doors. Men like trees live largely on air. Red corpuscles in the blood save one from the malady of seeing all things blue. A preacher must get away from his work one day in seven. Who is he that he thinks he can drive a coach and four through the Decalogue without paying the penalty? He should rest one month out of every twelve. If his church will not grant him this he should take it. No man can wear in the pulpit for forty years without periodic seasons for recuperation and repairs. There are men now fishing who catch no fish because they have never taken time to mend their nets. If a man makes a practice of preaching through his vacations, verily he has his explanations — and his reward.

Sometimes the despondency is the result of accumulated disappointments. The very finest spirits are often broken by the experiences through which a minister is called upon to pass. Every true workman wants to see results of his labor, but in the spiritual world tangible results are not always immediately forthcoming. If a man can see of the travail of his soul he will be satisfied, but it is hard to work by faith. The preacher does his best but the world does not budge. He preaches truth but hearts are locked and barred against it. Some men grow worse under his preaching, and even from the best of soil there come forth but puny and tardy harvests. For awhile he bears up under these cutting disappointments but at last his spirit flags and he falls headlong into a hopelessly dejected mood. By his voice and temper the world can see that he is a defeated and disheartened man.

Unless he gets out of this pit he is lost. Let him go to the New Testament and master the seed-law of the kingdom. Let him study the parable of the soils, a parable with worlds of consolation for preachers who are discouraged. Let him refresh himself with the thought that even when the seed is perfect and the sowing is faultless the harvest is often scanty or choked, and that from at least one variety of soil there can be no harvest at all. Let him ponder the parable of the harvest coming gradually, and rejoice in the assurance that the full corn is coming though his wistful eyes may see no more than tiny blades. The processes of spiritual development are slow but they are as orderly and certain as are the processes by which the universe has come to its present estate. It is a great thing to believe with one's heart and mind and strength that every bit of work done for God with patient hands and faithful heart is certain to bring forth some day, somehow, abundant harvests to his glory. No minister of Christ should rest content until this faith is his.

Many a man has been cast down by unreasonable expectations, and these expectations in numerous cases have been aroused by mistaken reading of the Scriptures. It is frequently asserted that if men will only preach the Gospel the crowds will flock to hear them, and as proof of this a sentence of St. Mark is quoted, "the common people heard him gladly." People who quote the Scripture ought to find out first what the Scripture means. On the day on which Jesus upset the Pharisees and discomfited the Scribes the common people, so Mark says, listened with delight. Of course they did. The Scribes and Pharisees were their hereditary foes. To see such snobs and pedants rolled headlong in the dust was to the common people an experience quite delicious. The words of Jesus were applauded with hilarity and glee. But outside of a few forlorn and forsaken sinners to whom Jesus' kindness was overmastering, what classes of people listened to him gladly when he was pressing upon the conscience high conceptions or arduous duties? For a little while the common people followed him because they took him for a Schlatter and a Barabbas rolled into one. As soon as they discovered he was not a Barabbas they had no further use for him, and cried, "Not this man but Barabbas!" The next time some one gravely quotes, "the common people heard him gladly," ask him, when? Certainly not in Nazareth for they tried to kill him there. Not in Capernaum for they deserted him there. Not in Jerusalem for they cried, "Crucify him! Crucify him!" Not on the cross for they wagged their heads and derided him. It is a monstrous perversion of the facts to say that the common people of Palestine accepted gladly the teaching of the Son of God. If they did why did he utter woes upon Bethsaida and Capernaum and Chorazin, cities filled with common people, and why did he sob, "O Jerusalem, how oft would I, but you would not!" And how did it happen that after three years of as hard work as a perfect man with perfect methods could do, assisted by twelve apostles and seventy heralds, he left at death a little company of only six hundred converts drawn from the millions of the common people in the midst of whom he had done his mighty works? The common people rejected both Jesus and his teachings nineteen hundred years ago and their temper has never changed.

Let no man then delude himself with the foolish expectation that the world is going to rush to hear him preach. The world has found Jesus out. It knows he is not a Barabbas nor a Schlatter, but a teacher of high ideals and uncomfortable commandments, whose disciples must not expect to be above their master and whose servants must be as their Lord. The New Testament makes it clear as light that we preachers shall have tribulation. If we live godly in Christ Jesus we must suffer persecution. We are sent forth as sheep in the midst of wolves. Unless we take up our cross daily we cannot be his disciples. If we are wise, we will accept this as our lot, not despondingly but with exceeding joy, desiring always that we may know Christ and his resurrection, and the fellowship of his suffering, being made conformable unto his death, if by any means we may attain unto the resurrection of the dead.

XI. The Value of a Target

But let no man rail at the soil till he has examined his soul. Obstacles without are as nothing compared with hindrances within. Men sometimes disparage their parish when they ought to be cudgeling themselves. "I have a hard field!" The good man sighs and on his sigh as on a rug lies down. The self complacency of some men is colossal.

It is easier to lose one's way in the ministry than in any other calling. Many a man gropes hither and thither like a traveler lost in a fog. The vastness of the world in which the minister moves renders it easy for him to be vague. Theology itself is a boundless science, but it is only one of many which closely touch the preacher's work. In the library as on the ocean one is lost without a compass.

The details of administrative labor are multitudinous, and a man unless clear headed will be swamped. A minister's work is of a routine character, and routine always tends to reduce the vitality of a propelling purpose. When the community expects a man to pray at stated seasons every week whether he is in the spirit of prayer or not, and at fixed intervals to give a discourse whether or not he has received a message, and to keep up this clock-like regularity straight onward through the years it is not difficult to see that the exercises which began as means to lofty ends may at last become ends in themselves. The prayer which once was winged with a definite aim may become a spoke in a revolving wheel from whose turning neither the preacher nor any one else expects results. The sermon which once thrilled with a burning purpose may dwindle into a display of verbal handiwork or a string of meaningless commonplaces with which to tie up a service. Even men who work prodigiously on their sermons may forget the end for which sermons ought to be prepared. To no one is sermon production easy, to many it is exhausting toil; and so intent sometimes does the worker become in the unfolding of his idea as to lose sight entirely of the work which the idea is meant to accomplish. The arrow is carefully and ingeniously fashioned and then shot at random into the air. The bullet is molded at great pains but no target is visible to the marksman's eye. Preaching which is if rightly done the most exacting and purposeful of all forms of labor may easily become the most desultory and purposeless of all.

This lack of aim works havoc in a parish. The man without a goal seldom gets anywhere. The leader who knows not whither he wishes to go, will land his followers in the ditch. A man is effective in the ministry, other things being equal, in proportion to the clearness of his purpose and the definiteness of his aim. This lack of intention reveals itself in the sermon. An aimless sermon breaks down the interest of a congregation and sends it home disheartened and confused. Men say to one another, "I do not know what he was driving at," — one of the saddest wails which ever escapes the lips of church attendants. Unless a man can make the purpose of his sermon stand out broad as a barn door he ought to go into some work for which the Lord has fitted him. The very mission of the pulpit is to fire men's hearts and set them moving out to battle, but if the trumpet gives an uncertain sound who will prepare himself for the conflict? Laymen frequently stand nonplussed at the close of a sermon not knowing what they ought to think or what they ought to do.

This target-blindness also discloses itself in parish administration. If a minister has nothing definite in his mind he is likely to organize a new society. There may be no need of it in the parish, and its creation may absorb vitality needed for the development of organizations already in existence, but to the clouded vision of a man without an aim a new society is always a thing to be desired, partly because it gives him opportunity to appear to be doing something when he is doing nothing and partly because a community is always ready to mistake the multiplication of wheels for an increased speed in the progress of the Lord's chariot. Probably half the organizations now in existence would never have cumbered the ground had it not been for the idle and fussy brains of men and women who care more for the manipulation of machinery than for the accomplishment of spiritual ends. Those whose heart is set on the attainment of definite results do not want to be weighted with unnecessary paraphernalia and desire as little machinery as possible.

A clear cut aim is the preacher's life-preserver. A preacher without a purpose is worse off than a man without a country. The frequent pondering of a purpose braces the heart and energizes the will. No question should be oftener on the preacher's lips than, "To what purpose is this?" That is the question with which he should begin every sermon. On the first page he should write in clean, terse Saxon the precise work which this particular sermon is intended to do; and on the last page he should write his honest answer to the question: Is this sermon so constructed as to be likely to accomplish the result for which it has been written?" The first and last pages of the sermon need not be given to the people, although if a minister has not the gift of clothing thought in garments of light let him help his people by telling them frankly at the beginning just what his sermon aims to do, and at the close let him condense into one compact and memorable sentence the gist of all he has tried to say.

To what purpose? That is an improving question for men who lead in prayer. It is a knife which prunes away superfluous petitions. There would probably be fewer skeptics in regard to prayer if ministers had not prayed so abominably. The man who goes into the pulpit to dawdle aimlessly through a long series of meaningless and unrelated petitions is taking God's name in vain.

If a clergyman has lost his purpose let him seek for it as for rubies and fine gold. When he finds it let him use it day by day. Let no meeting be held, no society organized, no new enterprise launched, no campaign entered upon, no sermon preached, no prayer offered without a sharp and serious pondering of the question, For what purpose is this? There will be a new consternation in the ranks of the army of the Prince of Darkness when a larger number of the captains of the Lord's host come to realize more fully the necessity of keeping one's eyes on the target.

XII. Building the Tower

A church likes to feel itself in the grip of a man who knows not only where he is going but also by what stages the goal can in all probability best be reached. Wretched indeed is the predicament of a congregation whose leader is a man with a higglety-pigglety mind and with no ascertainable ambition but to keep the sermonic mill grinding through the year.

A minister should live and move and have his being within the four corners of a far-reaching, constructive purpose. All his work should be done with an eye single to some one glorious end. Marvelous is the transfiguring powder of a purpose held firmly in the preacher's mind. Language cuts with a keener edge. Ideas burn with a hotter flame. Sermons, no longer isolated and unrelated, become confederates in a holy cause, joining hand in hand to pull down the strongholds of evil and lift men to the upper heights. Some men's sermons are only bushwhackers fighting a desultory and bewildered skirmish, other men's sermons sweep through the year like a well-disciplined battalion going forth to fight the battles of the Lord. To one preacher sermons are variegated beads loosely strung together on Sabbatic thread, to another they are constituent parts of an organic and growing whole. It is only when the sermons become connected chapters of a continuous story, the aim of which is clearly in the preacher's mind, that the heart-life of a congregation is symmetrically developed and the parish built up foursquare in righteousness.

Ministers of Christ are church builders and the architectonic gift is one of the most valuable of the gifts bestowed by the Eternal Spirit. A preacher should have the instinct and skill of the builder. What materials and in what quantity and in what proportions and at what times and in what places, — these are questions as important in spiritual church building as in the erection of structures of brick and steel; but they are questions which in many a parish are slighted or ignored. The Master said that any man about to build a tower ought first to calculate the cost. This preliminary investigation and estimate is an indispensable part of the work. The preacher is a tower builder but not every preacher seems to be aware of the fact. The most patent fact to some men is that two new sermons must be gotten ready every week. Like avenging furies these sermons drive their victims through the days and nights, and whether they will carry on and complete the work which preceding sermons have begun or prepare the way like John the Baptists for other sermons not yet arrived is a question for whose consideration the hurried hours allow no opportunity. A man thus harassed may become so absorbed in the work of preparing bricks and mortar for his tower that no time is left for the consideration of its architectural proportions or for a thought concerning the eternal laws in obedience to which all lasting structures must be built.

This lack of forethought and design is painfully apparent in many men whose gifts are conspicuous and whose success might be increased a hundred fold if they should form the habit of building the months and years into a plan. Such a habit systematizes the study and thought of the preacher and gives him a poise and power not otherwise obtainable.

It is the misfortune of many men that they fear to take hold of large things. Their texts and themes and outlooks and projects and problems are too small to develop themselves or inspire a congregation. A man may tempt himself by setting before him a block of five or ten years and saying to himself, "By the help of God I will carve out of this huge block of time the loveliest and greatest piece of work of which my powers are capable." By fixing his eyes not on next Sunday but on a Sunday ten years away, he will walk with a new tread under a new heaven and across a new earth.

Lift up your eyes then. Brethren, and take in the years which are to be. Every preacher ought to see clearly at least one year ahead of him. If he can see five, it is still better. If he blinds his eyes in the dust of the immediate present and allows life to become a haggard scramble for two new sermons for the coming Sabbath, he not only stunts his own intellectual development but dwarfs the spiritual stature of his church.

Every preacher should have a church year. This is well-nigh indispensable. If he does not like the one laid down in the books of the churches which retain the traditions of the fathers let him make one of his own. If he does not map out his scripture lessons in advance he will find himself reading the same passages again and again, passing over large sections of Holy Writ which his people need. It is only by painstaking planning that a minister can secure variety in his pulpit themes. Unless he takes time to recall his sermons of last year and to organize into a schedule the sermons of the coming year he will almost invariably cultivate some narrow field to which his own tastes incline him, ignoring wide domains of revelation which are never neglected save at the sacrifice of health and growth. He will fail also to present truth in its true proportions. There are certain facts of the Christian revelation which ought to be presented to a congregation every year. There are a few principles of conduct so central to Christianity and so vital to spiritual health that no year should pass without the preacher bringing to their unfoldment the united strength of all his powers. Without prearrangement these vital matters will be slurred or crowded completely out.

Not only are the phases of truth manifold but the methods of presentation are almost numberless. These should be employed in such a way as to give variety and refreshment. Some preachers are intolerably monotonous because they invariably appeal to the same faculties and deal always with the same type of doctrine. If they would sit down at the beginning of each year and make a careful diagnosis of the spiritual condition of their people, noting the dispositions to be curbed, the tempers to be nourished, the errors to be choked, the truths to be enthroned, the vices to be starved, the virtues to be cultivated, and then map out the year as a general outlines a campaign, appointing a definite number of sermons for the accomplishment of each particular design, and arranging the sermons in a sequence which will secure both continuity and momentum, and at the same time allow relaxation both to the preacher and the hearer by calling into exercise new combinations of faculties by the presentation of diverse but related realms of truth, he will not only find himself doing his work with increased facility and joy but he will see the spiritual life of his parish passing under his hand into those forms of beauty and power which he beheld first in vision and which by the co-operation of God are now embodied in the life of humanity to the glory of his blessed name.

XIII. Selfishness

The crowning glory of the character of Jesus was his unselfishness. "For their sakes I sanctify myself" — in this golden sentence of his high-priestly prayer is expressed the disposition which shaped his conduct from Nazareth to Golgotha. If it is essential that the servant be as his master and the disciple as his Lord, then to every minister of Christ there comes the call to sanctify himself for the sake of his congregation. It is for his people that the true preacher lives and labors. To serve them is his cardinal ambition, his consummate joy. By serving them he serves God. God and the people cannot be separated in the preacher's work. Thick-witted men occasionally get the notion that they can glorify God by preaching theology and at the same time scorn their congregation. By proclaiming in the pulpit unpalatable ideas in offensive ways they pride themselves on serving God no matter how they hurt God's people. Indeed a man may become so wrong-headed as to think that the farther he gets from his people the nearer he is to the Almighty. But if a man loves not his congregation whom he has seen how can he love God whom he has not seen? If a minister says he loves God, and in his heart slights or despises his people, he is not only a liar but a murderer of the spiritual life of his parish.

This neglect of the people on the part of the minister is more common than one likes to acknowledge. Selfishness may crop out in a man's vocabulary. Because a minister is familiar with the language of German philosophers and Scotch metaphysicians he may thoughtlessly use this dialect in addressing business men and farmers, servant girls and mechanics, uncaring whether they understand him or not. The man with the unselfish heart sanctifies his language for the sake of his people. He trims his sentences and simplifies his periods until his thought stands out radiant and compelling before every attentive mind. He makes himself of no reputation and takes upon him the form of a servant and is made in the likeness of a man. By humbling himself and becoming obedient to the law of the cross God highly exalts him by giving him access to the hearts of his hearers. A man of sympathy instinctively thinks of the limitations and needs of those with whom he deals. Paul always carried in his mind's eye the faces of the unlearned and the unbelieving. He insisted that a church service ought to be shaped with these people in mind. If they could not understand what was going on they could take no part in the service and might think Christians out of their head. He was hotly vehement in his denunciation of the selfishness which uses language that edifies the speaker but does not enlighten the hearers. In a burst of magnificent earnestness he says, "In the church I had rather speak five words with my understanding that by my voice I might teach others also, than ten thousand words in an unknown tongue." Would that this Pauline commonsense were abundant in all our pulpits!

The choice of themes often bears witness to this same deep seated sin. The true preacher lives for his people. To build them up is his supreme delight. For their sakes he shapes his reading and directs the main currents of his thought. Their aptitudes and attainments, their conscious wants and their unconscious needs stand before him day and night like so many angels of the Lord sent to tell him of what sort his sermons ought to be. But not every minister listens to these angels. Personal tastes are often followed, favorite lines of study are pursued with no consideration of the parish needs. Literary ambitions are cultivated and scholastic inclinations gratified in wicked disregard of everybody but the preacher himself. Such a man becomes a specialist and while cultivating his specialty his people pay the bills. They come to the house of God on the Lord's day hungry for bread, and instead of bread they receive a discussion of a tangled problem in sociology, or the elaboration of a distinction which struck the preacher's fancy in his reading of the last new volume on Ethics. It is advantageous and right for the preacher to have favorite studies and to set aside particular domains of learning for special cultivation, but over the gateway of this garden the words should be written, "For their sakes I sanctify myself," that both on entering and coming out of the garden he may be reminded of the obligation which surpasses all others and be saved from the selfishness which favorite studies so insidiously induce.

To persuade a clergyman to forsake his parish the Devil counts his greatest victory. If he can beguile him to scamper over the country giving his strength and time to miscellaneous audiences while his own people remain at home unshepherded and untrained, he wins a triumph over which the nether world rejoices. An English writer of note has said that the Devil in our day comes to ministers disguised as a railway train. He might have added that if a Pullman sleeper cannot catch a man, the printing press may. The prophet of the Lord may be seized with a mania for writing books. These books may have little relation to the Gospel or to the needs of his congregation, but the chapters of these books may be worked off on unsuspecting and defenseless saints as sermons. It has happened more than once that a preacher has allowed his pulpit ministration to be determined largely by the demands of his publisher. A man who perpetrates the chapters of his next book on his people not because his people need these chapters but because his publisher can use them, may excuse himself by saying that in his books he can serve a larger audience than could be assembled inside his church walls, but the average layman who has not debauched his conscience by any such sophistical argumentation will say that the man who receives a salary from one set of people for time and strength which he habitually gives to others, and who uses the pulpit simply as a source of supplies while engaged in a work other than that which he has promised to perform, is a shirk and a scamp even though he is a Doctor of Divinity and pursues his rascality for the avowed glory of God.

A minister owes much to his community, denomination, and country. The man who steadfastly stays at home refusing to turn a wheel or lift a burden outside his own little parish is the victim of a selfishness as loathsome as any of those above mentioned. Upon the Lord's wide work a minister must look with sympathetic eyes, and to many companies of brethren he must give himself as occasion offers with generosity and gladness. But he belongs first of all to his parish. The field in which he works is the world, and his church is the force with which he cultivates the field. To develop and consolidate this force and use it with increasing efficiency in subduing the world, this must be his supreme ambition, his constant study, his incessant care. To love his brethren over whom he has been appointed teacher and shepherd, this is the beginning and end of the whole matter. "Let us not then love in word, neither in tongue; but in deed and in truth."

XIV. Dishonesty

If an honest man's the noblest work of God, Satan's ignoblest masterpiece is a dishonest Christian minister. Nothing so undermines the confidence of laymen in their spiritual leader as the slightest indication in him of double-dealing. No sin is more deadly and degrading to a man of God than insincerity.

"That one error
Fills him with faults; makes him run through all the sins."

If a man is crotchety he can be tolerated; if he is prejudiced or ignorant he can be borne with; he may be lacking in a score of qualities which men count desirable and still be a useful and an honored man. But who can endure a minister who cheats or lies? The gospel preached by such a man falls dead and deadening. Prayer on his lips seems blasphemy. A religious service conducted by him exasperates every heart which doubts him. Deplorable is the condition of a church which has in its pulpit an anointed rogue.

Deliberate and cold-blooded liars are not numerous in the pulpit, but there are many men there who lack a fine and scrupulous regard for truth. The ethical sense even in ethical teachers may become strangely blunted, and men of noble gifts and lofty purposes have a curious fashion of doing unexpected and indefensible things. A minister's environment has a tendency to develop in him whatever germs of unveracity preceding generations may have bequeathed him. Many things are expected of him and it is human to shrink from disappointing expectations. He is expected to know everybody with whom he has ever shaken hands. To speak a blighting, "No," to a trustful, smiling individual who innocently asks, "Do you remember me?" seems an act of needless cruelty. The consequence is that there are ministers who remember everybody forever.

They read Paul's exhortation, "Lie not one to another" without wincing. A minister is expected to rejoice with everybody who rejoices and to weep with everybody who weeps, and it is the requirement of his office that he should give expression to these sympathetic feelings. Is it to be wondered at that his language sometimes becomes conventional and that his assertions occasionally have a hollow ring? To be deeply interested in a large number of human beings passing through a wide variety of experiences is possible but not easy, and men of narrow nature in using the broad and throbbing phrases of Christian brotherhood find themselves sometimes saying things which their heart does not follow. Human nature in many individuals is excessively fond of praise. Without it there is a coolness toward the church and preacher. How easy to pour the oil of adulation over the heads of these influential people until it runs down upon the beard even to the skirts of the garments! The habit of giving expression to genuine appreciation and merited commendation is both proper and lovely, but when politic adjectives and appeasing adverbs are scattered with a reckless disregard of truth, the preacher is securing an improvement in church climate at the sacrifice of his soul.

It is in these genteel and apparently unescapable ways that the minister receives his first lessons in departing from the truth. The departure once made other steps are not difficult. On going into the pulpit certain things are expected and the good natured man, always ready to oblige, proceeds to meet expectations. Ancient doctrines couched in traditional language will satisfy the men and women of light and leading, and so the ancient doctrines are elaborately set forth, though the minister if punctiliously faithful to his convictions would make considerable subtractions and sundry additions. To say precisely what one believes in a place consecrated to traditional interpretations and in the presence of people who are expecting statements to which they have grown accustomed is not easy.

There are not so many lying cowards in the pulpit as bitter critics see there, although the number is no doubt larger than it ought to be. Pulpit lying is generally of an unpremeditated and almost unconscious sort. There are clerical Munchausens who run a thread of romance through their sermons without the slightest compunctions of conscience. They have fibbed so long they cannot tell fiction from truth. These are the men who simulate emotions which they do not feel, and narrate events which never happened, and throw in exaggerations to heighten the effect, and tell what they thought, while on the Atlantic or the Alps although the idea first reached them in their study. All of these prevarications seem to spring out of a certain oratorical fervor rather than from the deep soil of the heart. This oratorical fervor is often responsible for lamentable behavior. Men become so zealous for the truth they lie for it. They misrepresent their opponents, and misreport what men of other schools of thought have said and written. It is hard for some men to controvert the opinion of another man without telling lies about him. In every season of theological controversy the amount of pious mendacity is incalculable. The heavenly treasures are indeed in earthen vessels.

But there is another form of dishonesty which seems to bear upon its forehead more unmistakably the brand of the pit. A man in the heat of discourse may run into statements which cannot be defended, but what shall we say of a man who deliberately lays his plans to deceive? Appearance rather than reality is still to many minds the one thing essential, and an occasional minister is ready to lend himself to the unholy work of making his church seem other than it is. Matthew Arnold has told us of our dangerous admiration for numbers, and in his essay he might have incorporated a paragraph with windows opening out upon the clergy. In an age which measures institutions not by spirit but by bulk, and which ranks men not by the fineness of their achievements but by the magnitude of their operations, a minister, if ambitious, is constantly tempted to increase the size of his church organization at the expense of its interior life. People are hustled into the church unprepared spiritually for its obligations and duties, and thus organized Christianity becomes weighted down with a mass of material which it is impossible to assimilate and difficult to cast out. Men who build into the temple of God hay and wood and stubble are the scourge of the modern church. The man who will inflate his church to impress the community by a display of figures is a man who will pursue dishonest courses to cover up a numerical shrinkage. Church rolls are often left unpruned for years, the names of the long absent and even the dead being jealously hoarded in order that steady and disheartening losses may be kept from public knowledge, and the preacher enjoy the reputation which a large church is supposed to give.

Brethren, be honest! Though the heavens fall, be honest! "The church exists," as Newman says, "not to make a show but to do a work." You are representatives of a religion whose fundamental virtue is sincerity, and the community has a right to look to you as men whose place is in the forefront of the age-long battle against all dishonesties and frauds and shams.

XV. Autocracy

A witty New Englander has given the world a fascinating sketch of the Autocrat of the Breakfast Table, but no one has yet given us a full length portrait of the Autocrat of the Communion Table. The Communion Table is used in this connection as a symbol of clerical prerogative. No one can touch it but a minister. Not even lay officials can take the bread and wine until they have passed through clerical hands. There is here a distinguishing distinction which lifts the minister above his brethren; and all distinctions, however justifiable and necessary, have a tendency to feed the pope which comes into the world with every man. The environment of a clergyman contains abundant nutriment for the nourishment of the papal proclivities of human nature. Not only is there a gulf between clergy and laity worn broad and deep in popular thought by the teaching of a thousand years, but a minister's work is of such a nature as constantly to give him the sense of importance and authority. Does he not speak for God? Is he not a successor of the Apostles? Has not a sacred charge been entrusted to his keeping? The very dignity of his work gives him a lofty mindedness which easily passes into pride and makes him exceeding jealous of all outside interference. Moreover, in his preaching no one is allowed to contradict him. No matter what he says the congregation sits dumb and acquiescing. Bitter protests may rise in the hearers' hearts but they fall back dead, strangled in the silence. If laymen were allowed to-day the privileges they enjoyed in the time of Jesus, and could say to ministers as they said to him right in the midst of the sermon, — "You are crazy! What do you mean by that?" church decorum would be badly mangled, but the minister would be saved from a temptation which like a beast now crouches at his door. The practice of presenting to people instruction on a variety of subjects without fear of open contradiction is apt to beget in any man who is not constantly on his guard a temper which Shakespeare takes off in the lines,

"I am Sir Oracle,
And when I ope my lips
Let no dog bark."

It is this immunity from contradiction on the Lord's day which renders many a minister so difficult to live with through the week. He cannot suffer opposition at any point in the entire circle of church administration. To differ from him is spiritual treason, to oppose him in any of his movements is to be a son of Belial.

It is this stripe of man who wants to run a church. He is sure to meet a layman who wants to run it too. And then —! But a church cannot be run by anybody except to its destruction. A church is an organism and like all organisms it refuses to be run. It will grow if carefully nourished and guided, but to run it is to wreck it. It is as delicate as a lily and as dependent on the law of freedom. The earth does not run the lily. It holds the lily tenderly by its roots and then gives it largest liberty to unfold in obedience to that mystic genius with which the lily is endowed. A church must receive nourishment from the preacher, but it is not for him to determine the shape of each petal or the precise length of its stem. Or to change the figure, a church is a family and a family cannot be run. Some men try to do it and the result is a tragedy which shows itself in the face of the wife and the disposition of the children. One can run a hotel but not a home. That home is happiest in which there is least visible constraint and most spontaneity and affection. A machine may be run but not a household, a business enterprise but not a church. Some men now in the ministry were evidently intended for engineers or managers of railroads and trusts. They cannot free themselves from the conviction that the church is a machine which they are to run along a track of their own devising to the destruction of every obstreperous layman who gets in their way. A church is a family and wise is the minister who is content to let it grow. It is for him to create the atmosphere in which the lovely things of the spirit shall come to their best estate. From him must come much of the energy by which the church fulfills the law of its being, but he will often do most when to onlookers he seems to be doing least. Happy is the man who has the faculty of so inspiring his church with the spirit of freedom and service that while he himself stands in the background the church apparently moves of itself into enlarging circles of spiritual culture and achievement.

It is a fatal blunder for a minister to make the decalogue and his own wishes equally binding on the consciences of his people. A preacher ought to prize with all diligence the men who differ from him and make use of their gifts up to the level of his opportunity. Every church ought to have in it men of all types of disposition and temper and opinion and culture and politics and theology. No one type ought to be suppressed in the interest of a deadening uniformity or for the purpose of securing universal harmony with the preacher. It is the business of a minister to make his church roomy. He must be the friend of the radical and of the conservative, of the orthodox and the heretic, of the zealous and the phlegmatic, of the sane and the crotchety, of the popular and the friendless, of the man who is with him and the man also who is against him, making himself all things to all men that he may do them good. For him to drive out the men who do not agree with his theology or politics, or refuse to fall in with his favorite enterprises, is to rob the church of its virility and originality and cripple it hopelessly in the work it aims to do.

A minister must learn to labor and submit. Cromwell's dictum is worth remembering, "In yielding there is wisdom." Even a good man is not infallible and the stars will not fall from heaven though the preacher fails to get his way. The things which a church ought to have will come to it not by pushing but by waiting. Horace Bushnell late in life said that could he live his life over again he would never push. The fable of the sun and wind making a wager as to their ability to compel a traveler to remove his cloak is not without significance for the man who would deal successfully with men. The minister who in order to induce his people to throw off habits or notions which he does not like, converts himself into a cold North-Easter, filling Sunday mornings with his icy blasts, will not succeed in the thing which he aims at and may possibly blow himself out of the pulpit.

XVI. Vanity

A writer of discernment has confidently asserted that all women are vain — and men more so. If ministers are not vain it is not because of any lack of provocation. A preacher's gifts are exercised in public places. He is pre-eminently a speaker and those who speak stand, as it were, on a pedestal, the observed of all observers. No matter how modest by native disposition the clergyman may be, publicity is thrust upon him, and if he be a man of gifts he stands perpetually in a golden shower of praise.

Every gift, no matter what it is, has a coiled serpent it. A man's deadliest danger lies ever at the center of his greatest strength. If a minister's most conspicuous gift is a rich and interpreting voice, then of his voice let him beware. Many a man has had his usefulness destroyed by the very gift which should have carried him on to power. The ability to utter sweet and thrilling tones may lead one into a habit of indulging in vocal parades full of music but void of the Gospel. It is doubtful if there is a more luxurious intoxication than that experienced by a man who, gifted with a voice of compass and passion, knows how to use it in mastering an audience. Not only do the tones soothe and entrance the hearers, they also mesmerize the speaker. Under the spell of his own utterance a man sometimes loses sight of his argument, and instead of working to lift his congregation to the level of a high ideal he falls to playing with his voice, tripping up and down the scale to exhibit its flexibility, exploding in thunder-claps to display its volume, rolling melodious modulations out over the heads of his hearers to test and exercise the marvelous organ with which a generous God has endowed him. Every acute-eared church goer has heard men preach who showed by their entire vocal behavior that, they cared less for their ideas than for their cadences and intonations. One cannot hear these elocutionary peacocks in their sermonic strut without wanting to cry out, "Quit your fooling and come down!" Sometimes the conceit is ridiculous to the verge of nauseating, for a man may be flushed over tones of which he has every reason to be ashamed. What spectacle more ludicrous and sickening than a man attempting with pompous mouthings to give expression to a message so sweet and simple as the gospel of that plain man of Galilee. If the men who indulge in starched and sonorous sounds with pompous self-complacency and amusing solemnity and fervor only knew how grotesque and silly their whole performance is they would throw aside forever their elocutionary airs and be content to be just sensible plain-spoken men.

All preaching rests upon a physical foundation. A commanding presence is a gift of the Almighty. "Big-boned men framed of the Cyclops size" have an immeasurable advantage over men of equal intellect but of slighter girth and stature. A handsome man in the pulpit woos and wins the eyes, and winning the eyes is almost half the conquest of the heart.

We are predisposed to listen to the messenger who comes to us with a majestic bearing. Some men subdue an audience before they speak a word. But this physical pre-eminence is not without its dangers. It raises expectations difficult to meet. When men look like Apollo we anticipate something divine. When they resemble Webster we demand that their thought shall match their looks. A dwarfed and bloodless sermon from a man with the mien of Jupiter is resented as an insult.

A glorious body may induce a vanity in its possessor which manifests itself in the form of self-confidence. Good looks will carry a minister far but not to the end of the day. A congregation can be impressed for a season by a massive body and by the ponderous tones of a commanding voice, but if the man in the pulpit is only a well-groomed animal repeating pious platitudes with the final tones of a Son of Thunder, he will early lose his church and find it hard to get another. Let all the pulpit Sauls beware! They are undoubtedly of the elect, but like their thin-chested, low-statured brethren, they must work to make their calling and election sure. A man of superb physique is under special obligation to fill his sermons with virility and mental fire. If because upon his body every god has set his seal to give the world assurance of a man of power, he becomes inflated and shirks the tough, hard toil which sermon creation inexorably demands, he is like the fool who built his house upon the sand. The storm is coming and there will be a fall.

Literary style is even more dangerous than good looks. The last has killed its thousands, the first its tens of thousands. Men too noble to be vain of a comely body succumb to the seductive power of success in using words. To speak and write one's language with elegance and precision is an achievement which rightly brings a sense of satisfaction. Expressing thought with distinction and grace is an art so difficult that men work for it as those who dig for hid treasures. With certain men the cultivation of style becomes a mania. For literary finish they are willing to sacrifice all the weightier matters of the law. Clearness and force and effectiveness they pass over as trifles, while they give tithes of the anise and cumin which grow in the garden of speech. It is not slander but truth to say that there are men now preaching the Gospel to whom the ideas of their next sermon are of less moment than the literary costume in which the ideas are to be dressed. These men wear their life out on their rhetorical finery, widening the fringes and multiplying the tassels, seeking like similar pedants of an earlier day, the praise of men, and not the honor which comes from God only.

But even these verbal fancy-work preachers have their admirers. No matter what a minister does some one is sure to commend him. No other man in the town is so praised as he. He may have a host of enemies but he is never without his friends. He may be criticised and abused, but he will also be complimented and flattered. No matter how poor his sermon some one will find in it the word of God and tell him so. His prayer may be feeble but some saint will thank him for it. Through the mail he receives notes of appreciation and thanksgiving. To some people he is surpassingly great. There probably never lived a preacher who was not to at least one soul the greatest man since Paul. All this is sweet and dangerous. To many it is fatal. Praise humbles some men, other men it spoils. They become conceited, lazy, reckless, unbearable. Puffed up by the eulogies of sentimental admirers they lose the vigor of manliness and degenerate into clerical fops. Popularity is the most fearful of all tests. If any man thinks he stands let him take heed.

XVII. Discontent

When Paul assured the Philippians that he had learned in whatever state he was therewith to be content, he confessed a higher state of grace than many of the successors of the Apostles have yet attained. Discontent may be said to be one of the prevailing sins of the ministerial world. How prevalent it is the public does not fully know, for ministers who are discontented do not shout their dissatisfaction from the house-top. They write it in bulky letters and send it in sealed packages to their ministerial brethren. The number of preachers now wishing a change of pastorate cannot be accurately computed, but if all the facts were known the world would be astounded. Men in the East, fretted by the stereotyped customs of fossilized communities, look with longing toward the West with dreams of the blessedness that must belong to ministers who can take a forward step without cracking their skull against a precedent. Toilers in the West, sick of the unchartered freedom of a population disinclined to submit to yokes either of God or men, wish themselves in the East where church-going is an established custom and life runs smoothly in channels made for it by the fathers. Preachers in rural places look with hungry eyes toward the city where pulpit gifts and graces meet with grateful appreciation, and preachers in one city look toward another city where the mountains have been apparently leveled, and the ways of the Lord have been made straight. Of a host of clergymen it may be said as one has written of the patriarchs, that they are strangers and pilgrims on the earth, and declare plainly that they seek a country.

In justice to the clergy it must be said that ambition is not generally the inciting cause of this restlessness. The popular impression that the average clergyman stands on tip-toe eager to heed the beckoning of the first parish which offers a larger salary or a softer bed of roses is as malicious as it is false. The explanation of the desire to escape from one parish to another may usually be found in the fact that ministers like other mortals do not like to be uncomfortable, and one sees fewer brambles in a garden which some other man has cultivated than in the garden in which one works himself. Every parish has in it men and women with whom it is difficult to live, and every church has problems which are a burden to the heart. Some men are so constituted that they cannot carry heavy burdens or face circumstances which prick like thorns. Their first impulse on the sight of any difficulty is to run. A man never knows a parish until he gets fairly settled in it. The years bring out the skeletons as the night brings out the stars. A few church skeletons are as terrible to a timid clergyman as graveyard ghosts to a small boy after dark. He may find to his dismay ancient quarrels which have been smoldering several generations and which at his first important movement blaze out in a conflagration which threatens to burn up the church. He may find a set of rogues in his official board, or a good-sized Pharaoh in the broad aisle. The church may be tied hand and foot by the pagan notions of a heathen clique, or the choir may be in a state of ferment sufficient to drive the spirit of devotion from every service. Gray headed men with antique ideas may frown down every suggested step of progress, captious critics may carp at his theology, rhetoric or necktie, Euodias and Syntyche may heat the atmosphere to torrid temperatures because they cannot be of the same mind in the Lord, prominent pew-holders may give up their pews and disgruntled workers may resign their offices, in short the church may have so many devils in it as to lead the unhappy preacher to question whether by any amount of prayer and fasting on his part the unhallowed brood can be cast out. A man in such circumstances may honestly wonder whether he is the one who is intended to redeem Israel or whether this particular parish ought not to look for another.

There are times when the trouble is the outcome of an evident misfit. When this is the case the minister should promptly shake the dust from his shoes, for there are other towns and cities in which the Gospel must be preached. But a minister should not too hastily conclude that because things are not altogether pleasant the Lord has need of him elsewhere. Unless the signs of an irreparable misfit are numerous and unmistakable the minister ought to set his hand resolutely to the plow and not look back until the furrow has been finished. It is not becoming in a prophet to run at the sight of trials. It shows fickleness of heart to accept a church and then drop it in the first fit of despondency. If he accepts the care of a parish in need of a surgical operation let him perform it and give the wounds time to heal before he turns the patient over to a new practitioner. Honorable men will not toy with churches. There is something of the sacredness of marriage in the pastoral relation and when once entered on it is for better or for worse. Short pastorates are unfortunate both for pastors and people. They develop in clergymen and laymen dispositions hurtful to spiritual growth. If a man knows he has but a short time in a parish he is tempted to do the things which are easiest and cheapest. He will not enter deeply into the hearts of his people but will be in danger of looking upon all laymen as so many pawns to be manipulated in an interesting game of ecclesiastical chess. It is the long pastorate which draws on the fountains which are deepest and which builds up in congregation and pastor those elements of character in which the New Testament exults and rejoices. A man who expects to live with the same people through many years will have every incentive to be sane and industrious, far sighted and true. He will not hesitate to enter upon schemes of education and training which can be completed only in long periods of time, and his life, blending more and more with the life of his people, will grow richer and fuller unto the perfect day.

Be content wherever you are, my brother, and whether you abound or are in want be not hasty to take up arms against a sea of troubles and attempt to end them by running away. For in that change of place what dreams may come and rough awakenings who knows! It may be your present parish is obscure, but blessed is the man with grace sufficient to grow in the shade. It is said that the chief reason why the sugar maple makes up a great part of the native forests of New England is that the maple is willing to grow in the shade. It is taking precedence of all other trees because a young maple is always in training ready to take the place of any tree which may die. Go to the Maple, young preacher, consider her ways and be wise. In a few years the great trees of the clerical forest will lie low, and your final place will depend in large measure on your present willingness to grow in the shade.

XVIII. Pettiness

Certain vices only mar, others lacerate and kill. Not one of them kills more surely than a petty disposition. Some weaknesses eat into the husk and bark of a man's life, but leaving the core untouched they do not fatally interfere with his preaching: but pettiness is a sin which blasts life at its center and takes out of preaching the spirit which gives power.

The Christian religion is nothing if not large. It spreads over us an infinite sky and throws around us horizons whose diameters cannot be measured. The men to whom it introduces us are large men, who revere the Maker and who have fetched their eyes "up to his style and manners of the sky." Their temper is heroic, their sympathy all-embracing, their spirit God-like. The ideals which hang before them shine as with the glory of celestial worlds and the motives which fire and impel their hearts are lofty as those which move archangels. At the center of this immortal company stands the man of Galilee from whose lips the minister must take his message and from whose heart he must draw the inspiration by which he is to prevail with men. Only a man of magnanimous spirit can be loyal to such a master and proclaim effectively so grand a message. A man with meager sympathies and stunted spirit may attempt to preach the Gospel but it will shrivel on his lips. No man truly preaches unless through him the truth can make its way, and if the channel is choked or narrowed the man may go on talking but a preacher he cannot be. A sermon is the life-blood of a man baptized into the spirit of the Lord, and every syllable of all he utters must have in it the weight of a full-statured Christ-like man. It is only words thus weighted which are able to find the blood. The Gospel from many a pulpit goes forth void because proclaimed by too small a man.

Pettiness sometimes manifests itself in penuriousness. Money stirs up strange fevers in the blood and in some men it creates a parsimonious disposition which is contemptible in any man and doubly so in a minister. It is no excuse for him to say that his salary is small, and that therefore he must pinch and screw, and haggle over the price of everything he buys. Poor men can be large-minded in money matters if they will, and it is always possible to be economical without being mean. Men of ability have thrown away their influence with their people simply by the display of a pickayunish, close-fisted disposition which rendered them despicable to all who had financial dealings with them. Business men can no more receive the Gospel from such a man than from the lips of a libertine or drunkard. Clergymen are as a class the most generous and self-sacrificing of all men, but if all secrets could be revealed it would probably be discovered that many a man while urging his people to be generous has forgotten the value of the contribution box to his own soul.

Pettiness takes many forms. It may crop out as envy and envy means impotence and death. Who can stand before envy was a question propounded by the philosophers of Israel and the answer is, No one, not even the man in whose heart the hateful sin has built its nest. It is rottenness in the bones, and any man afflicted with it will find his spiritual life crumbling down into a shapeless mass of ruins. Not all preachers can be equally talented or equally successful, and blessed is the man who can see his brother marching grandly on in advance of him and join in the hosannas which proclaim his coronation. Envy is a sin of weakness, and whoever is guilty of it confesses his inferiority. It is a viper which cannot fasten on the soul of a man genuinely strong. The only deliverance from its poison is a new infusion of the blood of him to whom desire for preeminence was and is and ever shall be ridiculous, and who is able to heal his heralds in these later times as he cleansed his disciples in the upper chamber on that great night when he used the basin and the towel.

This hankering for first place sometimes leads to something akin to insanity. It calls forth bursts of peevishness and childishness which bring a blush to the cheek of every manly-hearted man who is called upon to witness them. Some men are so conscious of their own rights, and so punctilious in regard to the payment of the pound of deference which the world owes them, that half the time they are in a huff because some one has unwittingly slighted them or refused to pay them the last farthing of etiquette which was their due. The date of the invitation, the affixes and suffixes, the place on the program, the rank in the procession, these certainly are not matters of life and death, but some men make them such to their own condemnation and the chagrin of their fellows. This touchiness often increases with age, and men with gray hair are sometimes guilty of a crochety and morbid insistence on trifles which stirs up in sensible people both anathemas and tears. The hoary head is a crown of glory if it be found in the way of righteousness, but when it is found in the way of babyishness the gray hair is only a bleached dunce-cap on the head of a fool. Some men cross the dead line in the pulpit early because they become in their interior life so insufferably petty and foolish. It was Goethe who said that as we grow older it is difficult to remain as wise as we were.

Occasionally this miserable disposition develops the poison of malice. The slight is too serious to be overlooked, the insult is too keen to be forgiven. And so the miserable man goes on preaching the New Testament with an unforgiven wrong rankling in his heart. Of all wretched mortals none is more to be pitied than the minister of Christ who attempts to preach the gospel with a quarrel on his conscience not yet made up and an enemy on his heart not yet forgiven. Such a spirit curdles the milk of the word, and reduces every sermon to a mockery. The poor man cannot open the New Testament without reading there his condemnation. He cannot read the Sermon on the Mount without stumbling over, "Leave thy gift before the altar, go and be reconciled to thy brother." He cannot read Peter's question, "Lord, how oft shall my brother offend me and I forgive him?" for the Lord's answer will loom up before him terrible as Elijah before Ahab at the gate of Naboth's vineyard. He cannot read Paul without receiving such dagger thrusts as "Be ye kind one to another, tenderhearted, forgiving one another even as God for Christ's sake hath forgiven you." He cannot read John's letters without being stricken down with such bludgeons as "He that loveth not his brother abideth in death!" He cannot even join his people in repeating the Lord's prayer without being dragged to the judgment bar by "Forgive us our debts as we forgive our debtors." A minister of the gospel of love who has an enemy whom he is unable or unwilling to forgive ought to repent or resign.

XIX. Foolishness

It was the opinion of the wise men of Israel that even though a fool be brayed in a mortar, yet his foolishness will not depart from him; and even men who are not fools often fall into forms of folly from which it is well-nigh impossible to deliver them. For instance, beginning a speech with an apology is a piece of nonsense unprovoked and inexcusable, but if you wish to break a man of that habit he must be caught young. There are ministers who seem incapable of giving an address without an elaborate explanation of their inability to do justice to the theme or the occasion. But why squander time in announcing what will become perfectly clear before one sits down? When a man is allotted a limited number of minutes in which to unfold an important subject, it is his business to begin at once upon his task and not squander people's time in wearisome explanations of his inadequate preparation or with egotistic intimations of the wonderful things he could do if he had only been given a fair opportunity. It was a shrewd reader of the human heart who said that an apology is only egotism turned wrong side out. But the apologetic devil has a method in his madness beyond the reach of reason. The larger the subject and the shorter the time, the surer is our excuse-making brother to enter upon minute lamentations over the limitations under which he must speak. When the program is extended and every moment is golden the explanatory dunce is at his best. It is then that he performs prodigies in the way of murdering time and multiplying words. Instead of plunging into his subject without a syllable of explanation and packing into the fleeting moments the solid gold of his thought he uses up the patience of his hearers and his own opportunity to prove himself a sensible man. Every theological student on his graduation day ought to paste in his hat the stern dictum of Emerson, "No sensible man ever made an apology."

This sort of tomfoolery may be carried into the pulpit where it manifests itself in long-drawn-out introductions, and exhausting preparations for great things which never come. If a man cannot say anything in the first ten minutes of his sermon he ought to drop the first ten and begin with the second ten. Even when the introduction is excellent it may be out of all proportion to the argument it leads up to. Building the porch larger than the house is a blunder peculiar to the builders of sermons.

It is at the beginning and ending that one is most tempted to waste time. Such expressions as, "In conclusion," "finally," "one word more," are forms of speech not only useless but full of mischief. What is gained by telling a congregation that the end is drawing near? When the "one word more" becomes like the widow's cruse of oil, the hearts of the faithful faint within them. A blunderbuss after saying, "Finally," is sure to catch a glimpse of a new idea, and straightway pursuing this, he will forget all about the promise he has made his hearers, and will go off on expeditions more extended than any ventured on in the body of his discourse. A sermon with two "finallys" in it is a monstrosity and a plague. Let the preacher speak right on with full momentum till he stops. On railway trains it may be necessary on approaching stations to whistle "down-brakes," in the house of God the sermonic train may be brought to an unannounced and instantaneous stop without fatality.

Humor is a rich gift of Heaven and fortunate is the man to whom it has been given in abundance. A little nonsense now and then is relished by all sorts of men, including preachers. Pleasantries and happy hits and jokes unstained and stingless, these are not unbecoming at proper times in a spiritual leader of men. But when a man is so full of funny stories that his stories are in greater demand than his sermons it is time for him to reflect. The ability to keep a dinner party in a roar is not to be despised; neither is the sobriety essential to influencing men in their attitude toward noble things to be neglected. Many a man in trying to be a jolly, good fellow has abdicated his position as leader of the higher life of his parish.

There is one sort of fun in which a minister should never indulge, and that is fun in which the Bible plays the part of the clown. A Bible sentence joked about becomes a withered leaf on the tree of life. The preacher can never use it for the healing of a soul in whose presence he has done his joking. Shallow and Godless men may indulge in stories and conundrums in which the words of saints and prophets are prostituted to the frivolous task of provoking laughter, but this is hardly proper for a man who is dependent on these very words for food supplies with which to feed the deepest hungers of his people. The noblest words are always most delicate and lose their bloom when played with by the tongues of punsters. A sentence of Christ may be so stained by the breath of laughter and so wrapped round with grotesque and sordid associations as to lose forever to the Christian the high and holy music with which it once came freighted to the soul. Many of us on looking through our Bible find sentences here and there which some joker in our presence once twisted into a lower meaning, and which can never be to us all they might have been had they never been blasted by a joke. A minister who sports with the Bible in the homes of his people need not be surprised to find them indifferent to its beauties when he invites them to study it on Sunday.

Men who shrink from the profane handling of the Scriptures do not hesitate, in many cases, to deal jocosely with noble feelings and lofty thoughts. There is a trick of passing from the sublime to the ridiculous, of reading frivolous meanings into stately words, of giving soaring sentences a downward twist, of dragging down high things to low levels, which is often cultivated because of the hilarity produced by it in circles incapable of appreciating higher forms of wit, but which when indulged in by the preacher is one of the most ruinous of blunders. There are ministers who have lost all helpful influence over the men who have come closest to them solely because of this fatal habit of cheapening the most sacred objects of thought by the profane sportiveness of the mind. The man who jokes straight through the week will be suspected of joking on Sunday. If he constantly reads ridiculous meanings into sober words in the presence of those who enjoy his intimate acquaintance, these persons will read jocose interpretations into the stateliest periods of his most earnest sermons. By acting the fool so constantly when out of the pulpit he will seem to be playing the same rôle even when preaching the crucifixion or celebrating the last supper. Alas for the man who is so incorrigibly and irresistibly funny that even in the pulpit he seems less of a prophet than a clown.

XX. Meanness

A modern John the Baptist has condensed his message to his generation into the pungent exhortation "Quit your meanness." It was the Scribes and Pharisees — the religious leaders of their nation — upon whom the ancient John the Baptist laid his hand with heaviest pressure, and possibly a few of their successors now alive would receive no milder treatment at his hands if he, returning from the dead, should subject them to the sifting, searching fires of eternal righteousness. When a minister of the

Gospel has a disposition to be mean he has unparalleled opportunities, and no other man is so shielded from rebuke. His ministerial brethren hesitate to reprimand him, his people mutter condemnations but do not strike. How to reach a mean man when once intrenched in a pulpit is indeed a problem.

Meanness is of divers varieties and shadings. Sometimes it is rough, raw boorishness. It is required in ministers that a man be found a gentleman, but the marks of gentle breeding are occasionally lacking. When a man seated in full view of an audience holds an animated conversation with his neighbor during the rendering of an anthem, or bustles from place to place attending to odds and ends of business when he ought to be listening to the solo, or fidgets and looks bored while another man is preaching, or holds up his watch and shuts it with a snap which sounds like a cannon-shot to the man who has not yet finished his address, he shows a lack of thoughtfulness and refinement which brings a blush to the cheeks of those who like to see in ministers a resemblance to that supreme Gentleman whose messengers they are.

This disregard of the rights of others often takes appalling forms. There are ministers who have no conscience in their treatment of the men who follow them on a program. If given the chance to speak first they take all the time there is, leaving those who come after them the raveled fragment of a ruined hour. A mental state capable of such conduct deserves the investigation of the psychologists. Why the work of preaching the Gospel should develop in certain minds the disposition of a brigand, and break down all fine scruples of equity and honor, is one of the problems for the new century. The facts are clear and incontrovertible. There are men of intelligence and piety who when asked to go with an audience one half hour will invariably go with it twain; who when asked to divide an hour with a brother minister will greedily devour the first half of it and take a huge bite out of the second; who will steal every moment they can wrap their tongue around, and then apologize to their outraged victim with the blandest of smiles, "I did not realize how long I was speaking!" A Christian worker who has had experience in the making of programs is inclined to think that if five speakers are wanted to grace an important occasion it would be safer to trust five men chosen at random from the penitentiary to do unto one another in the division of time the thing that is right, than five eloquent clergymen taken from as many Christian pulpits. This reckless overriding of all the proprieties and restraints is indulged in sometimes by men whose praise is in many churches, but the more conspicuous the offender the more lamentable the transgression.

Men who would not stoop to filch moments have been known to steal people. Denominationalism has flooded the world with blessings, but by intensifying rivalry among religious bodies it has led to evils not a few. The undue multiplication of churches within narrow boundaries sets ministers into competition with one another, and a sensitive man of honor sometimes finds himself outdistanced by a clerical rogue who uses underhanded methods to swell the number of his flock. Ecclesiastical fences are no longer high and some men are adepts in the knack of inducing sheep to jump from one field into another. Sometimes the work of proselyting is carried on slyly and with great adroitness, at other times it is prosecuted with boldness in the full glare of noon. Even men of dignity and undoubted piety have engaged in the unhallowed business, displaying among many graces of the spirit the strategy of the kidnapper and the cunning of the fox. But whenever and wherever and however and by whomsoever the work of building up one church by the tearing down of another is attempted the minister who lends a hand is guilty of one of the most contemptible and dastardly of all ministerial sins. What shall it profit a man to build up his church membership and lose his own soul?

This lack of principle sometimes crops out in a wanton disregard of the sacredness of a promise. The word of a minister should be as binding as his bond. Whatever he says he will do he should perform. Wherever he promises to go he ought to go. If the men who stand in the community as the anointed priests of conscientiousness and good faith say one thing and do another, to many men the pillared firmament will seem only rottenness and earth's base built on stubble. A minister of the Gospel is under everlasting obligations to be a man of his word.

But it is at this, crucial point that an occasional minister falls. There are men who are swift to promise and slow to fulfill. Invitations are accepted and then forgotten. Engagements are entered into only to be broken. With smiling assurances and fatal alacrity more work is promised than can possibly be performed. It is men of shining gifts who are most likely to be thus ensnared. Because talented they are incessantly and urgently importuned to give their time and strength to plausible and needy suitors. Because thus pressed they say, "Yes." After the invitation has been accepted there comes a new invitation, and this, for the moment more attractive than the first, crowds out its predecessor only to be shoved aside by a third invitation yet to come. Not a thought is given to the havoc thus wrought at the eleventh hour in the programs of innocent people who supposed it was safe to rely upon the promise of a clergyman; not a tear is shed over the mortification and ache of disappointed hearts. Fires of resentment are thus sometimes kindled in which one's primal faith in human nature is in danger of being consumed. One man of this stamp does more to undermine confidence in Christianity and its defenders than the arguments of a legion of infidels. His sermons will be but sounding brass and clanging cymbal to every man with whom he has dealt unfairly or to whom the story of his perfidy has been brought.

When a minister gives his promise let him keep it. Action must evermore keep pace with word. An engagement once made should be scrupulously fulfilled unless the Lord God Almighty raises up obstacles which no human ingenuity or strength can possibly surmount. If a minister cannot be a saint or hero, he can at least be decent.

XXI. Mannerisms

Every man must have a manner and when the manner is peculiar to himself it becomes a mannerism. Not every mannerism is offensive. There are tricks of gesture and of speech which because of their very oddity have a pleasing fascination, and seem to be a fitting and completing part of a man's own personality. They give us in fuller measure the aroma of his soul. But mannerisms as a rule are veritable dragons which throwing themselves between the preacher and his hearers must be warred against and slain. Eternal vigilance is the price the man of God must pay for deliverance from this plague of pulpit pests.

There is scarcely an organ of the body which will not enter into conspiracy to cripple the minister in his work. His eyes may roam above his hearers' heads or dart periodically toward the floor, or hang themselves to a peg in one corner of the room, or shut themselves up as if afraid of the light, or stare steadfastly into vacancy like the eyes of Macbeth on beholding the dagger, refusing to do what all sane eyes are intended to do — look an audience in the face. His nose, if unregenerate, may sniff and snort, punctuating the glad tidings of great joy with indescribable sounds which are hardly fit music for the House of the Lord. His face may break loose from all restraint and indulge in grimaces wonderful to see. It may look solemn as death when there is no reason for solemnity, and wrathful when there is no call for indignation, and amused when there is no justification for mirth, and it may twist itself into contortions which if reproduced by the kinetoscope would furnish interesting diversion for the ungodly. Or his entire head may become unmanageable, wagging and wabbling, jerking and bobbing, as though ideas are nails which must be driven in by the skull used as a mallet. The hands also may become unruly, cutting capers behind their owner's back, fumbling and twitching, grasping and groping, expending nervous energy which ought to be poured into the voice. Or bolder in action they may gambol incessantly before the eyes of the congregation, doubling themselves into fists when the sermon is breathing the spirit of peace or pounding the unoffending pulpit until the exhibition of physical vigor makes a deeper impression than the unfolding of the spiritual idea. Some men get more dust out of the pulpit cushion than light out of the text. The legs may prove recreant to their trust. They may bend at the knee at every downward gesture of the arm, or one leg may run away from the other and lounge about in slovenly attitudes. The very toes may behave unseemly, lifting the preacher up and down, increasing and shortening his stature, giving the congregation the impression of a man unstable in all his ways. As there are kickers in the pews so are there men who kick in the pulpit. To some ministers the most effective of all exclamation points are those made by the boot.

But no matter what absurdities and crudities a minister's body may be guilty of, these can be endured providing the good man can manage his mouth. "Whoso keepeth his mouth and his tongue keepeth his soul from troubles," and also saves his congregation from a multitude of woes. If a man clears his throat at the end of every fifth sentence there will be persons in his congregation who will want to clear it out of the pulpit altogether. If he hems and haws whenever an idea gets away from him he irritates both his throat and the nerves of his people. If he yells at the top of his voice in the utterance of feeble ideas he is a nuisance which ought to be abated. When finely organized Christian men and women cannot attend church without receiving a headache from the stentorian tones of the preacher it would seem that yelling, like other forms of sin, ought to be made a cause for church discipline. If a congregation were a colossus to be attacked by rhetorical bludgeons, or a mammoth baby to be tickled by vocal pyrotechnics, or a monster to be tricked and trapped by oratorical devices, yelling might not be without justification: but as a congregation is nothing but a big, sensible man waiting to be spoken to by a little man in the pulpit, anything in the nature of a howl from his lips is as vulgar as it is absurd.

But a yell is scarcely worse than a tone. A tone is a clerical whine, a pulpit twang, an oily, sanctimonious, vocal monstrosity. A tone is cant vocalized. It is affectation coined into breath. It is the most disgusting sound which the universe emits. It is better that a minister should be afflicted with yellow fever than with a tone. With the yellow fever he might die. Some ministers have several tones, one for the prayer, one for the Scripture, one for the sermon, and still another for religious conversation. They talk like Mr. Hyde in the pulpit and like Dr. Jekyll at the foot of the pulpit stairs.

"O for a looking-glass for the voice!" This has been the cry through the centuries, and in the fullness of time there came the phonograph. What part in the evolution of the clergy this little instrument shall play it is too early to declare. But the courage and fidelity of the phonograph prove that it is an angel of the Lord. Before its arrival no preacher could hear himself as others heard him.

This metallic angel insists on telling the whole truth without the suppression of a vocal jot or tittle. If the minister smacks his lips at the end of paragraphs especially delicious, if he clips his "ings" or hisses his "esses," if he smoothers his vowels or magnifies his consonants, if he meters his sentences or builds a sing-song into his climaxes, the faithful phonograph will tell the round unvarnished story, and it will tell it without apology or compunction. The story may bring bitter tears, but if they lead unto repentance the world will find another man willing to preach the Gospel in the tones in which men are born.

Probably no defect of public speech is so common and so difficult to cure as the habit of monotony. There is a monotony of pitch, another of force, another of rate, another of inflection, another of emphasis, another of cadence, and the speaker who is not in any way monotonous is one man picked out of ten thousand,

To Hercules undying honor has been given because he accomplished twelve stupendous labors; but the minister who can meet and conquer all the lions, boars, and hydras which infest the road which leads to effective speaking is a mightier hero than the laureled demi-god of Greece.

XXII. "Thy Speech Bewrayeth Thee."

Discontent with theological seminaries is one of the conspicuous phenomena of our time. The discontent expresses itself often in blind and vindictive ways, and men and methods are struck at which merit only praise. But when congregations prefer men — as they often do — on whom the Seminary has not left its mark, it is not because congregations are perverse or stupid, but because they instinctively feel a difference in men which, however difficult to define, is no less real and controlling. In some cases it is sheer native ability which more than compensates for lack of scholastic straining, but in more instances it is a difference in speech which causes one man to be chosen and the other left.

The greatest danger to which a young man is subjected in the Seminary, is not, as many timid folks imagine, heretical interpretations of the Scriptures but a style of language which the plain people do not understand. The Seminary is a world of itself, and in this little world a dialect is spoken which one does not hear on the streets. The books which the student reads are written either in German or French, or in English almost as "foreign" as either. The lectures to which he listens are couched in terms which, however expressive and delicious to the trained scholar, have little meaning to the unlettered. No part of a man is more sensitive to his surroundings than his vocabulary, and one naturally speaks in the language with which his ears and eyes are most familiar. Unconsciously to himself the student acquires a vocabulary and a diction totally different from those which belonged to him in earlier years, and which will be a serious barrier to him in his efforts to reach the hearts of men. Many a man has come from the seminary with his vocabulary so Latinized, and his style so Germanized, that though his heart still beat in sympathy with the common people he seemed to them a foreigner or pedant.

The first essential of effective preaching is that every man shall hear it in the language in which he himself was born. No Pentecosts have ever been, or can ever be where this condition is lacking. No man truly preaches who does not reach the heart, and language is the instrument by which the heart is reached. Learning is good, but it is not essential. People care nothing for learning in preachers unless much else goes along with it. What is demanded is a man capable of communicating thought and feeling. If the preacher throws over his ideas thick verbal veils, and muffles his feelings in sentences which quench their heat, the congregation may call him learned but it will not care to hear him preach.

Next to the baptism of the Holy Spirit the most indispensable gift for every American preacher is a mastery of the English tongue. No time should be begrudged spent in the perfecting of the preacher's style. Language is the tool' with which he does his work, and it is a tool which demands a deal of toil. Any style is good which does its work. The work of the preacher is to make glorious to the hearts of men the facts and principles of revelation in order that by this vision they may be impelled to a closer walk with God. The first thing that a preacher must demand of himself is that he shall be understood. Unless he is understood all is vanity and vexation of spirit. His words should be clear as crystal and his sentences should shed light. His paragraphs should cut like swords and flash like torches. His language should be what John Milton said the best poetry ought to be, simple, sensuous and impassioned. The sermon should be free from opaque and clouded phrases, and should abound in "words which the heart knows." The preacher's aim is to move the will. To do this he must stir the emotions. His language therefore must be the language of the conscience and the heart. His style must be pedestrian. It must fit down close around the skins of things. If he weights his sermons with technical and abstract terms he becomes insufferably tedious and heavy. Hundreds of good men are failing in the pulpit to-day because handicapped by their language.

Let every man who wishes to preach with conquering power work in season and out of season on his style. It is a lifelong enterprise and no other labor is more profitably expended. The advice of Charles Lamb to Coleridge, "cultivate simplicity" is almost as important for the preacher as any statement in the Sermon on the Mount. Preachers as a rule are not simple enough. They imagine that deep thought and big words must go together. Let them read the first chapter of John's Gospel. No profounder piece of composition was ever written, and most of it is in monosyllables. "All of your sermons should be of the simplest," said Martin Luther to a growing preacher, and all successful preachers have acted on that advice.

Bookish words which have not been domesticated in the speech of the average member of the congregation ought to be avoided. The great words are nearly all short words, God and man, heaven and home, wife and child, life and love, faith and hope, joy and grief, pain and death, all these and a hundred like them drop easily from the tongue. The words which lovers know and which mothers speak in soothing and instructing little children, and which fathers whisper in the chamber of death and sob beside the grave, and which all men use in carrying on the life and business of the world, are all simple words, and these are the words which should be most frequent on the preacher's lips. These words are stained through and through with the heart experiences of many generations. They carry with them a light and fragrance which fill all the room in which they are spoken.

"He to whom the world's heart warms
Must speak in wholesome, home-bred words."

Foolish is the man who discards all these for the frigid patois of the latest literary or scientific school.

But a clear and moving style is not to be had for the asking. It is an attainment bought by most men by agony and sweat of blood. A man must feed his vocabulary constantly or it will lose its vigor and ardor. The vocabulary of a minister is subjected to a tremendous wear and tear which soon leaves it impoverished unless constantly replenished. A preacher's style should be full of color and music. Faded and threadbare language is not fit raiment for the message of the king. Too many preachers use a language which is colorless and tasteless and dead. There are no vivid adjectives, no picturesque phrases, no paragraphs which give fresh splendor to familiar ideas. A minister must deal constantly with moral commonplaces, but these become irksome and revolting unless expressed in language which has on it the dew of the morning. Love must always say the same things, but it never repeats itself.

How can a man freshen and enrich his style? Read and reread the Bible and Shakespeare and Defoe and Swift and Bunyan and Tennyson, for all of these have a genius for pouring the water of life into the clay jugs of Saxon speech. But reading is not enough. A man must himself be simple and true. Schopenhauer is right in thinking that "style is the physiognomy of the mind, and a safer index to character than the face." Whatever tones up the spirit and cleanses and sweetens the heart imparts straightforwardness and vigor and bloom to a man's speech. The purest, noblest English ever written is that of our King James's Bible. Its unfading glory is no mystery to those who have come to know the beautiful and saintly soul of William Tyndale.

XXIII. Books and Reading

There are preachers who would be stronger in their ministry if they read fewer books. There is every provocation to read too much. Books are numerous and cheap and no other working man in the town has so many hours in a week which can be given to reading as the minister. Even if he had no taste for reading he would be driven to it by the nagging question hurled at him from every side, "Have you read ____?" A man who values a reputation for being up with the times hesitates to say "No" more than half the times the question is asked him. Moreover it is pleasant to talk about books. Minister and people can come together on common ground in the books they have all been reading. But a parish gulps down an enormous amount of printed pabulum in a calendar year, and the minister who tries to read everything his people are reading is in danger of fatty degeneration of the mind. When he passes from his parish into the circle of his ministerial brethren he is pelted with another set of interrogations which call for acquaintance with an entirely different set of books. His brethren have read the last six volumes from Germany and the latest twelve from England and two or three from France, and the ambitious man, anticipating the discussion which is coming has also read them every one. A minister is thus spurred on by the world, the flesh, the devil, and the saints to swallow a larger mass of printed material than his mental stomach can digest.

A loud, long warning should be sounded against the intemperate use of books. It is commonly taken for granted that reading is of necessity a blessing; not infrequently it is a curse. A reader of many books is counted wise: his reading may make him a fool. Many a man would be saner, stronger, more effective in his work had he read but a fraction of the books to which he has given strength and time. This habit of omnivorous reading begets mental habits which are blighting to the preacher's work. Men addicted to it often become painfully superficial. By the constant skimming of ephemeral volumes they become incapable of constructive and continuous thought. They are men of thoughts but not of thought. To string thoughts together is one thing, to develop a thought is another. Men best versed in the thoughts of other men may become shallow in their own.

This superficiality sometimes displays itself in a mania for quotation. Every book is pounced upon for the sake of the homiletic material it contains and this is thrown into the sermon as a substitute for thinking which the preacher should have done. By the skillful weaving together of striking sentences from a group of miscellaneous writers a preacher may gain among ignorant people a reputation for vast and varied learning, but to the discerning he is not so learned as he seems. A sermonic crazy-quilt of purple patches may furnish entertainment and even instruction for a season, but preaching such as this does not furnish the solid and nutritious food which growing souls demand. If "preaching is the bringing of truth through personality" then the incessant lugging in of the ideas of other men must be a destructive if not fatal blunder; for it must of necessity check the flow of the preacher's soul upon the hearts of those who hear him. Men are best helped not by being told what the preacher has been reading, but by having poured out upon them the hopes and convictions which have become so vital in his heart as to shape themselves into a message which must forthwith be uttered.

Reading makes a full man and it may fill him to his undoing. One may be so full as to become incapable of effective utterance. Men sometimes degenerate as preachers in proportion to their advance in the realm of learning. While building increasingly spacious barns in which to store their sermonic goods a mental paralysis steals upon them, and in the day of plenty they find themselves unable to feed the souls entrusted to their keeping. The constant dumping of miscellaneous material into the mind breaks down the powers of assimilation, and leaves the gourmand a mental wreck. The juices of the mind dry up, and instead of a man behind the pulpit there is only a library bound in human skin. No human being can be so stale and flat and unprofitable as a man who has lived too exclusively with books. A sermon which smells of the lamp can be endured but never enjoyed.

Excessive reading may ruin a man as a preacher and also as a pastor. The love of books like the love of wine may grow until it becomes a consuming fire in which all obligations are burnt to ashes. When a minister neglects the sick and dying, when he ignores the stranger and the man in need of counsel, when he goes toward his people with repining and returns to his books with a sigh of relief he has entered on the road which leads down to the chambers of death. For it is his spiritual manhood which is in process of disintegration. He is losing the temper without which no man can be a true servant of Christ. Such a man becomes increasingly fastidious, dainty and critical. The more he reads the less he knows and so he reads still more. With accumulating knowledge comes a loftier standard. This higher standard renders him increasingly impatient with himself and especially with his brethren. He becomes unsympathetic, censorious, conceited. He measures every man by his scholastic and literary yardstick. Better men than he who have a different kind of knowledge obtained by other methods become to him only objects of pity or derision. No pride can be more scornful and cruel than the pride of a man who has lived with his books until he has lost his sympathy with men. But with all his learning he is wretched and miserable and poor and blind and naked. "Killed by his books" would be an epitaph fitting for the tombstone of many a ruined prophet of the Lord.

But books must not be undervalued. Alas for the congregation whose minister has ceased to read. Men who would grow must be diligent students of the best books. They will not read every book of which one hundred thousand copies may be sold but will shut themselves up with the supreme books, the literature of power. These books will be reread many times. Benjamin Jewett in one of his letters says he had just completed the fiftieth reading of Boswell's Johnson. It is not advisable to give exclusive attention to technical studies even though they relate to the Bible. The work of tracing tendencies, and spotting interpolations, and detecting redactors is interesting but debilitating. Let the man of the pulpit read poetry for language and vision, biography for impulse and comfort, history for proportion and perspective, and the Bible for fire. He who keeps constant company with the kings and queens of human thought will have a keenness of insight, a delicacy of touch, and an energy of persuasion which his indolent, newspaper-magazine-novel reading brother may envy and marvel at but never possess.

XXIV. Near to Men Near to God

It is not good for a man to live alone. He belongs to humanity and only in close relation with his fellows does he realize the life for which he was created. The highest virtues and sweetest graces grow only in an atmosphere made warm by human fellowship. Isolation, like a blighting frost, nips spiritual aspirations in the bud. A man may be a pagan alone, he cannot be a Christian. It is where two or three are together that Christianity promises a life which is divine.

A preacher of Christianity must live as close as possible to men. Isolation to him is fatal. If he has a disposition which shrinks from the society of others his disposition must be born again. Young men in whom the literary instinct is strong and the literary ambition stronger still, sometimes enter the ministry determined to be strong — as they say — in the pulpit, and suppose that it is by the constant poring over learned volumes that pulpit greatness can be achieved. Shutting themselves up in their study they proceed to dig in a dozen different fields of learning, leaving untouched the very field in which the pearl of great price is hid. It is with reluctance that they lay aside their books to go among their people and every hour given to parochial visitation is bitterly begrudged. Among their books they are serene and happy: among God's children they are restless and forlorn. By pampering this disposition a man may come at last to have a horror of entering the homes of his people and may secretly despise the very souls he is sent into the world to love.

Knowing men is the preacher's first and most important business. To know them he must be with them. It is not enough to know man, he must know men. He can study man in his library but he must study men in his parish. It is one thing to know human nature as portrayed in books and another thing to know it at first hand. Europe in books is not more different from the Europe which the tourist sees and hears and feels than is the man whom we read about different from the man whom we meet in the streets. It is the man in the street whom the preacher must know, and if he does not know him no other sort of knowledge will make him a successful preacher. There are two volumes to which a preacher must give his days and nights, his Bible and his parish. A knowledge of the second is not a whit less important than is a mastery of the first.

According to the New Testament the minister is a servant. His rank in the kingdom is determined by his proficiency in service. A man who desires to be "great" in the pulpit must be first of all a minister, and if he has an ambition to be chief he must be the servant of all. If a preacher really deserves to serve his people he will not count time lost which is spent in their company. The closer he comes to them the larger his opportunity to give them what they need. What they are fearing and hoping, feeling and thinking, enjoying and suffering, loving and hating, reading and dreaming, all this can become known to him only as he comes into contact with them, and to know these things is more important than to know nine-tenths of all the books can teach. It is because men love to luxuriate in the "quiet air of delightful studies," and "to suck the sweets of sweet philosophy" or are ambitious to shine as oratorical or literary stars that they come to underestimate the value of pastoral visitation and place a knowledge of books above the love of men.

But it is for the preacher's own advantage that communion with his people may be most strongly urged. He needs the people even more than they need him. As a preacher he is maimed unless he have warm and tender sympathies, and how are these to be maintained unless he lives close to men? Men who aim to keep the Godward side of their soul open while the manward side remains shut aim at the impossible. It is the fundamental doctrine of the New Testament that we approach God only through humanity. According to Jesus right relations with man precede all the forms of worship. According to John we know we have passed from death to life only when we love the brethren. If the world is to know that men are Christ's disciples because they love one another then a minister's self-denying affection for his people is the one supreme test of his right to be counted a faithful servant of the Lord.

From his parish he will glean ideas and also gather nutriment with which to feed all his powers of feeling. One half day spent close to ordinary mortals will give a man more clear and helpful thoughts than can be found in the last learned book, no matter who the author. Men are better any day than books. They are written all over by the finger of God and happy the man who can read this living revelation edited down to date.

If a pastor neglects his people for his books he pays dearly for his sins. Not only does he lose that keenness of sensibility and tenderness of sympathy which give sparkle and warmth to the sermon, but like a man who has lost his way he wanders in a realm of ideas foreign to the lives of his people. His vocabulary will sound like that of a man from far off regions. By his mouth he is condemned. He may try to induce his congregation to believe that he cares for it but the telltale words with which he builds his sermons will cry out against him. Worst of all he will have in his own heart a hunger which is never satisfied, and will find the satisfactions of the ministry grow less with the increasing years. The joy of life lies in one's relations with his fellowmen. If a minister is not taking his people deeper into his heart and if he is not constantly growing deeper into theirs his life will grow increasingly monotonous and he will be likely to be one of the notorious one hundred who apply for every vacant pulpit. To sit in one's study grinding out great ideas, that to a young man seems the road to pulpit greatness; but in later years he learns that pulpit greatness is not the knack of playing with ideas but the power of expressing a loving message in familiar words and throwing around it an atmosphere of fire. In short it is the gospel of love which the preacher is most in need of. Not until he loves is he truly born of God. "In the government of nations," said Cromwell, "that which is to be looked after is the affection of the people," and no less is true in the government and leadership of churches. A recluse may by unusual gifts of speaking, win a short-lived admiration by extraordinary pulpit feats, but it is the man who sincerely loves his people and who is sincerely loved by them who most surely moulds their temper and turns their feet into the way of life.

XXV. Eagles, Race-horses and Plodders

The climax of God's redeeming grace, according to Isaiah xl., 31, is found in the strength which enables men to plod. To soar like an eagle is difficult, to run like a race-horse is more difficult still, but to walk and not faint — this is the greatest feat which the power of God can enable any man to do.

The high art of walking is one which the minister must master. Of all men he can least afford to indulge in the luxury of flying or running. These only put him out of breath and unfit him for his work. His usefulness depends upon the evenness and continuousness of his labors. He is a shepherd and shepherds neither fly nor run. A shepherd's work is prosaic, tedious, slow and obscure. Feeding sheep is his daily task and for this he needs neither the mettle of the racer nor the buoyancy of the eagle. He must have a genius for plodding. The clergyman who is able to trudge bravely through the years, filling the months with quiet honest work, pressing himself close upon his people and holding his people and himself close to the heart of Christ may cause little stir in the world but he will make an impression which will be felt in heaven. The farmer and preacher have need of the same patience, fidelity and pluck. The laws of the soil and the soul are inexorable and processes of growth in matter and spirit are orderly and slow. There must be hard plowing, faithful sowing, patient waiting, and skillful harvesting if the Lord of the Harvest is to give a reward. A man who only prances or flies is a failure both in pulpit and field.

But this gift of plodding has not been given to all men. It is a form of genius, almost as invaluable and rare as that of the artist and poet. If a man does not possess it let him keep out of the ministry. He will be unhappy all his days and at eventide it shall be dark. The parish will be a cage against whose bars he will beat and bruise his impatient wings; the church will be a dray in whose shafts he will chafe and fret, repining always over imaginary races which he might have run and won.

Some men cannot brook obscurity. They covet popular attention. They live on public favor. Unless they can attract and hold the eye of the community they are of all men most wretched. To be ignored by the press is to them Gehenna. To glorify God and enjoy him forever is not enough: they must cut a figure along with other notorious characters in the public eye, for this also is a part of the chief end of man,

And so instead of going quietly about their work doing good to all men according to their opportunity, they attempt to play the eagle. They soar into the heavens of dazzling rhetoric, and spread their wings in the broad realms of sensational devices. To make a show either in the pulpit or in parochial activity becomes a consuming, devastating ambition. These would-be eagles of the pulpit have brought the clergy in many quarters into irretrievable disrepute. Not a few newspaper men hold ministers in contempt because of their unhappy dealings with pulpit eagles who have clamored incessantly for the privilege of soaring in their columns. A minister itching for public recognition not only makes himself ridiculous but throws suspicion on all his brethren. Or if a man is too shrewd to thrust himself upon the lords of the press he may display his eagle instincts in other ways. He may prepare "great" sermons — possibly three or four — just to let his people know what tremendous heights he can reach when he cares to spread his pinions. But these aerial flights use up so much vitality that for a month after one of them he is as tame and weak-winged as an aged barn-yard fowl. No man can fly all the time or even one day in seven. And worst of all this mad desire to imitate the eagle begets and nourishes a deep-seated discontent. The man afflicted with it is always brooding over imagined slights and neglects. The community does not appreciate him, his own church underestimates his ability, and out of this sense of injustice proceed vague and feverish dreams of other parishes where eagles are appreciated at their full value, and of other people whose eyes are open to the gifts and graces which his own people fail to see. It is the misfortune of ministers who want to fly like eagles that most of them have only the wings of a more humble bird. What seems to them august soaring appears to those who behold them nothing more than the awkward flopping of a gander which does not know his place.

To be a clerical race-horse is as disastrous as to be an ordained eagle. Some men are always running races and attract the public notice by their snorting and perspiration. They look upon all the ministers around them as so many rivals in a race, and laying aside every weight — sometimes even ethical obligations — they run with fury the race which is set before them, looking not unto Jesus but at the man who seems most likely to outstrip them. This race becomes more furious if the ministers chance to be of the same denomination, for in that case the speed made by the racers will be entered on the same page in the denominational church record, and a clergyman stands branded in the eyes of church committees who is unable on the race-track to leave all Competitors behind. Sad indeed is the story if one had the heart to tell it. What will ministers not do when the fever of the race-course is once in their blood? They will lie about the size of their congregations and pad the roll of their church membership, and drop subtracting insinuations about the man ahead of them, and carry into the pulpit a heart full of envy and bitterness, and become a hypocrite as deep-stained and damnable as were the hollow-hearted miscreants at whom the Lord hurled thunderbolts nineteen centuries ago.

The salvation of the minister like that of other men lies in his willingness to do his duty without fuss or feathers up to the level of his strength and opportunity. Fame is nothing, publicity is nothing, popularity is nothing, serving God by helping men is all. Most of the best work done in the world is done by unnoticed toilers in obscure fields. Most of the best preaching is done in pulpits which have no halo around them in the public eye. The best sermons do not as a rule get into the papers, nor is any mention made of them by the reporters. The most influential preachers are not those most talked about but those whose words go deepest into the consciences and hearts of men. The church can afford a few eagles and race-horses of the nobler sort, but after all the solid and enduring work must be done largely by the plodders. My brother, if you are capable of walking without fainting, thank God and take courage. You are a man of gifts, and have in yourself indubitable evidence of the presence and favor of the Almighty. Other men may astonish the nation by flying over every celebration, but at the end of the day you having sown precious seed will come home rejoicing bringing your sheaves with you.

XXVI. Unconscious Decay

It is the nature of many of the most vital and transforming of the spiritual processes to take place below the reach of consciousness. A man growing better does not measure the stages of his progress, nor does a man becoming worse realize the headway of his descent. There are things which are hidden from the vision of both saints and sinners. Their eyes are holden so they cannot see them. Thus Moses after his long communion with the Eternal came down from the Mountain with a glory on his face, but "Moses wist not that his face shone." What was evident to others was concealed from him. Likewise Samson after that the Spirit of the Lord had departed from him "wist not that the Lord was departed." This awful fact did not break upon him until by the failure of doing things which formerly he had done with ease he found himself impotent and humiliated in the presence of his foes.

The processes of life and death run on to-day held in the grip of laws established at the beginning, and many a Moses illumines his people with a glory of which he himself does not dream, while many a Samson with great deeds behind him still marches boldly against the Philistines not realizing that the spirit of the Lord goes with him now no more.

It is for this reason that many of the professional apostles of the so-called higher life do not win the confidence of the discerning. They talk too much. The man who says, "Look at me, see how my face shines!" closes our ears to his argument for holiness by the impudence of his vainglorious invitation. Self consciousness and lofty spiritual attainments do not go together. Men who live nearest to the heart of God do not prate of their visions nor boast of the light in their face.

We cannot fail to be suspicious likewise of the Samsons who lose the power of conquering but in their weakness go on boasting as if they were still able to carry off the gates of Gaza. Because a man is once a preacher it does not follow that he is always a preacher. A man may lose his heavenly credentials although he continues to write "Reverend" in front of his name. The descent to Sheol is easy and for the minister as for all mortals the way is always open. It is not closed on Sundays and no broader entrance opens into it than from the pulpit platform. It is the truth even as Father John has written it, "our old man is constantly present with us, tempting us, snaring us, corrupting us, destroying us." The deterioration of spiritual life in men ordained to preach the Gospel is one of the saddest of all the mysteries of sin. Like Judas men for a while cast out devils and then fall by a devil themselves.

Always some one besetting sin lies at the root of the tragedy. The wages of sin is death in all circumstances and generations. Ministers escape exposure longer than most men because their sins are in general sins of the spirit rather than of the flesh and hence bring only spiritual retribution. They who sow to the flesh reap corruption. Gluttony and drunkenness and licentiousness — these sins are evident going before to judgment, but these are not the sins which entrap and slay the leaders of the church. Ministers, with rare exceptions, fall by the hands of enemies no less fatal but far more insidious and respectable, pride, selfishness, envy, covetousness, laziness, ambition, these and a host of others. The sinner is not exposed to sudden and spectacular ruin, he dies piece-meal. Unconscious of the progress of the processes of moral disintegration he suffers as the paralytic suffers by a progressive loss of sensibility and power. Who does not know ministers of the Gospel who once were favored and mighty men and of whom the world now says, How are the mighty fallen! They are still in the pulpit but their usefulness has ended. Their sermons are sounding brass and worse. Their prayers are useless as the prayers of the priests of Baal. What they say has no influence on their congregation, for their voice has lost the subtle and commanding accent of spiritual veracity. When one comes to know these men in the privacy of their own personal life the cause of the decay of spiritual power becomes clear. They are ministers but they are not good men. They are petty or niggardly or stingy or lazy or censorious or pretentious or pessimistic or sour. The light and joy have gone out of their own soul and therefore power has gone out of their preaching. Their failure in the pulpit is to them a mystery, but it is not a mystery to any one who knows them and understands the conditions of spiritual power.

The dead-line then is a terrible reality which ministers of all ages need fear and shun. Some men die earlier, others die later, the date is determined by the rate of progress of their sin. Only a man genuinely good can be a minister of power to the end of the day. All others are sooner or later overtaken and overwhelmed.

Nothing is more tragic than the spectacle of a minister who began his career with men eager to hear him, preaching at last to a world unresponsive to his message. The world to such a man is an insoluble enigma. Why he should fail while other men succeed is a tormenting problem. He compares himself with his successful brethren and in no whit does he seem to fall behind the chief of them. He has gone through college, and completed a Seminary course, and read shelves of books and studied elocution under a dozen teachers, and therefore why should he not succeed? He frames his diplomas and reads over his ordination papers. These are regular and valid and therefore wide doors of usefulness ought to open. He compares his sermons with those of men to whom the world seems glad to listen, and in illustrations, ideas, rhetorical finish, logical force, homiletical art, his sermons are fully equal and in many points superior to all. He picks up the name of a favored preacher and says, "Why should his name be sounded more than mine? Speak them, mine doth become the mouth as well. Weigh them, mine is as heavy. Now in the name of all the gods at once upon what meat doth this our Chrysostom feed that he is grown so great!" Poor man, he has left out of consideration the one thing essential — the spirit of God. It is not by rhetorical might nor by logical power but by the breath of the Spirit that congregations are swayed and the gates of the kingdom thrown open. And this only a good man can have. Sermons are like salt; they have a color and texture and weight, but all these are as nothing unless there goes along with them a savor. If the sermons have lost their savor, no matter what may be their rhetoric or logic or thought they are good for nothing but to be trodden under foot of men. For ministers then as well as for laymen the words of the Hebrew preacher have abiding significance.

"Fear God and keep his commandments,
For this is the whole duty of man."

THE END

www.ingramcontent.com/pod-product-compliance
Lightning Source LLC
LaVergne TN
LVHW050941080826
845145LV00004B/1358

* 9 7 8 1 7 8 9 8 7 5 7 8 2 *